T0208768

WHY
ANOTHER BOOK
— ABOUT —
BASEBALL?

L CHADWICK BOWMAN

author HOUSE®

AuthorHouse™
1663 Liberty Drive
Bloomington, IN 47403
www.authorhouse.com
Phone: 1 (800) 839-8640

Published by AuthorHouse   06/16/2020

ISBN: 978-1-7283-6472-8 (sc)
ISBN: 978-1-7283-6471-1 (e)

Print information available on the last page.

Any people depicted in stock imagery provided by Getty Images are models, and such images are being used for illustrative purposes only.
Certain stock imagery © Getty Images.

This book is printed on acid-free paper.

Because of the dynamic nature of the Internet, any web addresses or links contained in this book may have changed since publication and may no longer be valid. The views expressed in this work are solely those of the author and do not necessarily reflect the views of the publisher, and the publisher hereby disclaims any responsibility for them.

I grew up in a little place in south central Oklahoma where you spent summer playing baseball in the local church leagues. My brothers and I played for Bray Missionary Baptist Church at Bray. That was long before Little League took over. We played in the Marlow Church League. I mention this because this is where I got the love for baseball. My father was a baseball fan and taught all his kids, girls too, about the game.

In school at Bray Public School you played baseball and basketball, if you were a boy, girls just had basketball. I came from a family of 10 children, 4 girls and 6 boys. Nine of the ten grew to adulthood. There was 23 years difference from the first child to the last. Exactly 23 years. I was born on my oldest sister's 23rd birthday. Lucky girl. The reason I mentioned her was because she had a step-son a two years older than me, Louis Halford that I played baseball with every summer and we both collected baseball cards. When we couldn't play ball we played games with our cards.

From this came my love for more than playing the game. I loved statistics, reading where the players were from, how many were all-stars, or played in the World Series. I would listen to the Cardinals or Astros on the radio at night (it was tough when they were on the west coast). I remember taking the radio, after asking permission, to school so we could listen to the World Series. Remember, night games didn't start in the Series until 1971.

I recall the 1967 series between the Red Sox and Cardinals. I was a Cardinal fan, Bob Gibson, Lou Brock, Tim McCarver, and the rest was my team. I also liked the Red Sox though. Yazstrzemski, Petrocelli, Aparacio, Howard, and the rest. Gibby won 3 games and Brock stole 7 bases as the Cards won in seven games. A classic. In 1968 the Cards played the Tigars. In game one, Gibby broke Sandy Koufax's strikeout record for a single game and Brock stole 7 more bases in the series. Kaline, Northrup, Freehan, McLain, Lolich, and the other Tigers would win in seven games. Lolich would outduel Gibson in game seven for the win.

It was this love for baseball that I decided to write this book. Things I learned, remembered, saw, heard, and read. I want to share with other baseball fans and drive an interest to those who don't share my love for the game. My dream was to one day play in the majors, but I accepted that I wasn't good enough. I also wanted to be an announcer and sports reporter. I finally got to be a reporter at Konawa, Oklahoma for their football and basketball teams. Coleman, Oklahoma baseball and basketball, too.

I would do anything to be a part of baseball. I coached little league in Duncan, Oklahoma, Coleman, Oklahoma, and Caddo, Oklahoma. I worked as an umpire for little league baseball and softball in Bray. Then I umpired high school for five years, but heart problems forced me to give that up.

Then I started coaching softball, slow pitch and fast, for several years. It was fun, but not baseball. I enjoyed coaching in all phases though. I was an excitable coach, to say the least. I once threatened to use a bat on a punk for running over my catcher, a 15 year old girl. I was never thrown out of a game, but came close. As an ump, I tossed only one person, a coach, from Konawa.

This book is all mine. I put what I want in here and only what I want in here. You will not find any praise or worship of Ty Cobb or Cap Anson. Both hall-of-famers, but they were raciest, bigots, and dirty players. Cobb once said he didn't like niggers, Jews, wops, dagos, spics, or Indians. Anson took his team to play once and the opposing team had a black catcher, Moses Fleetwood, and Anson told the opposing team if the nigger plays we won't. Commissioner Kenesaw Landis was also a raciest. Now I've got a problem with the fact that these men are still in the Hall. Pete Rose can't be inducted because he bet on his team. So did Cobb, but being a friend of Commish Landis bailed him out. Barry Bonds, Mark McGuire, Roger Clemens, Sammy Sosa and other are not getting votes because they used PERFORMANCE ENHANCING DRUGS (PEDs).

Baseball was losing its fans, popularity, after going on strike, but a homerun race changed all that. When McGwire, Sosa, and Ken Griffey Jr started a race for 61 all of America tuned in. Especially when it turned to a two man race, Big Mac and Slammin' Sammy. What a race. Then along came Bonds to shatter McGuire's record.

I understand that PEDs may let a man hit the ball harder and throw it harder, but it don't give them eyes to see or quickness to swing nor control to throw. I was once an opponent to these guys, but now I say "Let them in". Rose is the greatest hitter of all-time, Bonds the greatest long ball hitter, Clemens one of the greatest strikeout pitchers. If we can allow raciest bigots in the Hall then let these guys in too. Or take out the haters. You would be surprised how small the Hall would become.

If I could time travel I would go back and watch these sport stars: (1) Jim Thorpe, playing ANYTHING, (2) Satchel Paige in his prime, (3) Chief Bender, (4) Jim Brown not only a football star, but lacrosse too, (5) Pete Maravich, (6) Honus Wagner, (7) Jackie Robinson playing ANYTHING, (8) Jesse Owens, (9) Negro League Baseball, (10) Women's Baseball League, (11) Babe Didrikson play ANYTHING, (12) Jim Shoulders, (13) Cool Papa Bell, (14) Yogi Berra, (15) Christy Mathewson, (16) Nolan Ryan, (17) Bob Feller, (18) Larry Mahan, (19) Gail Sayers, (20) Barry Sanders, (21) Wilt Chamberlain, (22) Don Meredith, (23) Nadia Comaneci, (24) Walter Johnson, and (25) Bob Ueker. Okay, that last one was a reach, but I'd love to sit by him for one game.

If you have a complaint about how I feel or what I write all I can say is, "Write your own." I just want people to enjoy this book and somewhere say "WOW, I didn't know that." Please enjoy and share what you learn.

BASEBALL TEAMS

BRAVES
1876 – 1882 Boston Red Caps, 1883 – 1906 Boston Bean eaters, !907 – 1910 Boston Doves, !911 Boston Rustlers, 1912 – 1935 Boston Braves, 1936 – 1940 Boston Bees, 1941 – 1952 Boston Braves, 1953 -1965 Milwaukee Braves,1966 – Present Atlanta Braves

CUBS
1876 – 1889 White Stockings, 1890 – 1892 Colts, 1898 – 1901 Orphans, 1902 – Present Cubs

PHILLIES
1880 – 1882 Worcester Brown Stockings, 1890 – 1941 Philadelphia Phillies, 1942 Phil's, 1943 Phillies, 1944 -1945 Blue Jays, 1946 – Present Phillies

GIANTS
1883 – 1884 Gotham's, 1885 – 1957 New York Giants, 1958 – Present San Francisco Giants

CARDINALS
1884 – 1891 Browns (American Association), 1892 – 1898 Browns, 1889 Perfectos, 1900 – Present Cardinals

PIRATES
1887 – 1889 Alleghenies, 1890 Innocents, 1891 – Present Pirates

DODGERS
1890 – 1898 Bidegrooms, 1899 – 1910 Superbas, 1911 – 1913 Dodgers, 1914 – 1931 Robins, 1932 – 1957 Brooklyn Dodgers, 1958 – Present Los Angeles Dodgers

REDS
1890 – 1943 Reds, 1944 – 1945 Red Legs, 1946 – 1953 Reds, 1954 – 1960 Red legs, 1961 – Present Reds

ATHLETICS
1901 – 1954 Philadelphia Athletics, 1955 – 1961 Kansas City Athletics, 1962 – 1967 A'S, 1968 – 1986 Oakland A's, 1987 – Present Athletics

INDIANS
1901 – 1902 Bluebirds (or Blues), 1903 – 1911 Naps (after Napoleon Lajoia), 1912 – 1914 Molly McGuires, 1915 – Present Indians

ORIOLES
1901 Milwaukee Brewers, 1902 – 1953 St Louis Browns, 1954 – Present Baltimore Orioles

RED SOX
1901 – 1907 Americans, 1908 – Present Red Sox

YANKEES
1901 – 1902 Baltimore Orioles, 1903 – 1912 New York Highlanders, 1913 – Present Yankees

WHITE SOX
1901 – 1902 White Stockings, 1903 – Present White Sox

TIGERS
1901 – Present

TWINS
1901 – 1905 Washington Senators, 1906 – 1956 Nationals, 1957 –
1960 Senators, 1961 – Present Minnesota Twins

ANGELS
1961 – 1964 Los Angeles Angels, 1965 – 1996 California Angels,
1992 – Present Anaheim Angels

ASTROS
1962 – 1964 Colt 45's / Colts, 1965 – 1997 National League Astros,
1998 – Present American League

METS
1962 – Present

RANGERS
1962 – 1971 Washington Senators, 1972 – Present Texas Rangers

BREWERS
1969 Seattle Pilots
1970 – 1997 Milwaukee Brewers (American League)
1998 – Present Milwaukee Brewers (National League)

NATIONALS
1969 – 1995 Montreal Expos
1996 – Present Washington Senators

PADRES
1969 – Present

ROYALS
1969 – Present

MARINERS
1977 - Present

ROCKIES
1993 – Present

MARLINS
1997 – 2000 Florida Marlins
2001 – Present Miami Marlins

DEVIL RAYS
1998 – Present

DIAMONDBACKS
1998 - Present

NEGRO LEAGUES

ST LOUIS STARS, CHICAGO AMERICAN GIANTS, DETROIT WOLVES, HOMESTEAD GRAYS, KANSAS CITY MONARCHS, PITTSBURGH CRAWFORDS, TRUJILLO ALL STARS, WASHINGTON ELITE GIANTS, BALTIMORE ELITE GIANTS, PHILADELPHIA STARS, INDIANAPOLIS ABC'S, ST LOUIS GIANTS, TOLEDO CRAWFORDS, INDIANAPOLIS CRAWFORDS, NASHVILLE ELITE GIANTS, NEWARK DODGERS, BALTIMORE BLACK SOX, and NEW YORK CUBANS.

BASEBALL THEME MOVIES
YOU NEED TO SEE

There have been six "baseball" theme movies nominated for Academy Awards. That is where will start this list:

(1) PRIDE OF THE YANKEES, based on the story of Hall of Fame Yankee LOU GEHRIG. It starred Gary Cooper as Gehrig, nominated for Best Actor; Teresa Wright, Best Actress nominee; also nominated for Best Picture, Best Original Music, Best Writing, Best Sound Mixing, Best Visual Effects, Best Story, Best Art Direction, and Best Cinematography. It won Best Writing Adapted for a Screen Play,

(2) THE NATURAL, Featuring Robert Redford, Robert Duvall, Glen Close, and Richard Farnsworth. Close won Best Supporting Actress, it also was nominated for Best Cinematography, Best Art Direction, and Best Original Score.

(3) IT HAPPENS EVERY SPRING, A comedy starring Ray Milland and Jean Peters. Won a nomination for Best Story

(4) THE FIELD OF DREAMS, starring Kevin Costner, James Earl Jones, Burt Lancaster, and Amy Madigan. Nominated for Best Picture, Best Adapted Screenplay, and Best Original Music Score,

(5) BANG THE DRUM SLOWLY, with Robert De Niro, Michael Moriarty, and Vincent Gardenia who won Best Supporting Actor

(6) BULL DURHAM, Nominated for Best Original Screen Play, it starred Kevin Costner, Tim Robbins, and Susan Sarandon.

THE NEXT LIST IS BIOGRAPHICAL MOVIES

(1) THE BABE RUTH STORY starring William Bendex and Claire Trevor

(2) THE STRATTON STORY starring James Stewart and June Allyson

(3) THE WINNING TEAM featuring Ronald Reagan and Doris Day

(4) THE JACKIE ROBINSON STORY with Jackie Robinson and Ruby Dee

(5) PRIDE OF ST LOUS starring Dan Dailey and Joanne Dru

(6) FEAR STRIKES OUT with Anthony Perkins and Karl Malden

(7) MONEY BALL WITH Brad Pitt and Jonah Hill

(8) A LEAGUE OF THEIR OWN with Tom Hanks, Gena Davis and Lori Petty

(9) THE ROOKIE starring Dennis Quaid, Rachel Griffiths, and Angus T. Jones

(10)   42 starring Chadwick Boseman, Harrison Ford, and Nicole Beharie

(11)   61* starring Barry Pepper and Thomas Jane

(12)   COBB with Tommy Lee Jones

(13)   DON'T LOOK BACK with Louis Gossett Jr, Beverly Todd, and Cleavon Little

(14)   EIGHT MEN OUT with John Cusack, Charlie Sheen, and D B Sweeney

(15)   ONE IN A MILLION starring Levar Burton and Madge Sinclair

(16)   A WINNER NEVER QUITS starring Keith Carradine, Ed O'Neil, and Dana Delany

(17)   CURVEBALLS ALONG THE WAY featuring Paul Sorvino and Robert Loggia

THEN THERE ARE
DOCUMENTERIES TO WATCH

(1) KEN BURNS' BASEBALL

(2) SIGNS OF THE TIMES

(3) TOP OF THE 10th

(4) LIFE AND TIMES OF HANK GREENBURGH

(5) MANTLE

(6) TED WILLIAMS: AMERICAN HERO

(7) I SEE THE CROWD ROAR

(8) THE GHOST OF FLATBUSH

SOME OTHER GOOD MOVIES

(1)   FOR THE LOVE OF THE GAME

(2)   MAJOR LEAGUE (all three)

(3)   TALENT FOR THE GAME

(4)   LONG GONE

(5)   MR 3000

(6)   ELMER THE GREAT

(7)   ALIBI IKE

(8)   KILL THE UMPIRE

(9)   THE SCOUT

THERE ARE LOTS OF GOOD READING OUT THERE HERE ARE A FEW AND WHO THEY ARE ABOUT

(1)   LET'S PLAY TWO, Ernie Banks

(2)   THE OLD CUB, Ron Santo

(3)   PLAY HUNGRY, Pete Rose

(4)   SON OF HAVANA, Luis Tiant

(5)   FROM GHETTO TO GLORY, Bob Gibson

(6)   IMPERFECT, Jim Abbott

(7)   THE CONTRACT, Derek Jeter

(8)   BOYS OF SUMMER, Roger Kahn (about the Brooklyn Dodgers)

(9)   BIG TRAIN, Walter Johnson

(10)   DON'T LOOK BACK, Satchel Paige

(11)   THE LIFE OF HENRY AARON

(12)   CHIEF BENDER'S BURDEN

(13)   A LEFTY'S LEGACY, Sandy Koufax

(14)   THE LIFE, THE LEGEND, Willie Mays

(15)   FALL FROM GRACE, Shoeless Joe Jackson

(16)   BASEBALL'S LAST HERO, Roberto Clemente

(17)   EDGAR, Edgar Martinez

(18)   DOC, Dwight Gooden

(19)   CHIPPER JONES, BALLAYER

(20)   JUST SHOW UP, Cal Ripkin Jr

(21)   BALL FOUR Jim Bouton

(22)   CATCHER IN THE WRY, Bob Ueker

(23)   VEECK AS IN WRECK, Bill Veek

(24)   ME AND THE SPITTER, Gaylord Perry

(25)   BASEBALL IS A FUNNY GAME, Joe Garagiola

(26)   THE BRONX ZOO, Sparky Lyle

LITTLE THINGS YOU MAY, OR MAY NOT, HAVE KNOWN ABOUT BASEBALL

(1) Dick Redding was dubbed, "the Cannonball", and was a very effective pitcher in the early Twentieth Century. Some of his highlights: (A) In 1921 he outduel Carl Mays in a 15 inning complete game 2-1 victory, (B) he shutout the Braves in a 10 inning complete 1-0 game win, (C) then dueled Grover Cleveland Alexander to a 2-2 tie in 14 complete innings, and (D) the year after Babe Ruth had hit 59 homers, he struck out the Mighty Bambino 3 times.

(2) Monty Stratton was a talented pitcher who lost a leg due to a hunting accident, BUT still pitched.

(3) Pete Gray lost an arm as a boy while trying to jump on a train. He still played baseball in the MLB.

(4) Bob Gibson played with the Harlem Globetrotters.

(5) Gabby Harnett missed only three foul balls in 1,990 games as a catcher.

(6) Jim "Catfish" Hunter threw a perfect game in 1968 and it was the first in the American League since 1922.

(7)   Walter Johnson tossed five Opening Day Shutouts, his fifth
       he won in 13 innings 1-0

(8)   April 14, 1993 Brewers pitcher Graeme Lloyd and catcher
       Dave Nilsson became the first Australian pitcher/catcher
       combo in the same game in MLB.

(9)   Gabby Hartnett is in the BASEBALL HALL-OF-FAME,
       PRO FOOTBALL HALL-OF-FAME, and NCAA FOOTBALL
       HALL-OF-FAME.

(10)   In 1945 the Washington Senators had only one homerun at
       home all season.

       It was an inside-the-park homerun.

(11)   In 1953 Mickey Mantle hit a blast measured to be 565 feet,
       at Senator's Griffin Park.

(12)   In 1930 the Phillies led the league in batting as a team with
       a .315 average, but finished in in last place in the league.
       Their pitching staff had a league worst 6.71

       ERA.

(13)   In 1962 the New York Mets last 120 of 162 games.

(14)   In 1982 Rickey Henderson stole 130 bases to set a MLB
       record.

(15)   In 1982 Rickey Henderson set a record for most times being
       caught stealing a with 42.

(16) Pie Traynor batted .356, 108 RBI's, and 540 at bats. He struck out only 7 times

(17) In the seventh game of the 1966 World Series Jim Palmer threw a shutout over Dodgers when he was nine days shy of his 21st birthday making him the youngest man to do so. He out pitched Dodger Hall-of-Famer Sandy Koufax, who appeared in his last game that day,

(18) Harvey Haddix, on May 26, 1959 threw a perfect game for 12 innings, but lost in the 13th inning.

(19) On April 27, 2005, Mark Grudzielanek became the player with the longest name In MLB history to hit for a cycle.

(20) In 1999 a 35 year old high school baseball coach named Jim Morris jumped to the major leagues as a relief pitcher (The Rookie).

(21) In 1952, Hoyt Wilhelm, a twenty nine year old rookie pitcher, hit a homerun at his 1st at bat. In his second at bat he tripled. In 20 years he never hit another of either one.

(22) In 2001 when he won the Rookie-of-the-Year season, Albert Pujols played in games at four different positions (1B, 3B, RF, and LF)

(23) The worst shutout beating a team ever took was a 22-0 win by the Pirates over the Cubs on September 16, 1975

(24) In 1982 the Cardinals won the World Championship while hitting only 67 home runs, dead last in MLB.

(25) 1n 1991 the Expos played 93 games, of a 162 game schedule, on the road due to damage to Olympic Stadium

(26) Once, Dodger Hall of Famer Don Newcombe refused to throw batting practice so Manager Walt Alston told him to "take off his uniform and go the hell home".

(27) The 1911 A.L. homerun leader was Frank Baker with 11. He was called Homerun Baker despite having only hitting 96 career dingers.

(28) King Kelly once inserted himself into the lineup in time to catch a pop foul next To his team's dugout.

(29) In the 1890's baseball was plagued by "rowdyism" or dirty playing and physically attacking opposing players, opposing fans, and, even, umpires.

(30) In 1966, the Reds considered Frank Robinson "over the hill" and traded him to the Orioles. In 1967 Robinson won the batting title with a .316 average, the runs batted in title with 122, and the homerun title with 49, therefore winning the A.L. Triple Crown and, also, was named MVP.

(31) In the original rules of baseball, pitcher gave the catcher the pitch signs.

(32) The pitcher had to throw the ball where the batter indicated where he wanted it. Thus the reason batters stick the bat over the plate.

(33) Gloves were not worn

(34) Pulling the ball was discouraged

(35) As was hitting fly balls

(36) The pitcher threw whenever he was ready

(37) The first "star" player to wear a glove was Albert Spaulding. Yes, that Albert Spaulding. He would later leave baseball and start a sporting goods company.

(38) The 1869 Reds were awarded a trophy bat with CHAMPIONS engraved on one Side and all the player's names on the other side. The bat was 27' long, 19" at the barrel, and 9 ½" at the wrist.

(39) The first bats did not have knobs at the end of them. Babe Ruth designed the first bats with knobs so he wouldn't lose the grip on the bat.

(40) The first World Series was played in 1903, the second in 1905. There wasn't one played in 1904, because the Giants refused to play the Red Sox.

(41) The 1870 Reds played 57 games, winning 56 and 1 tie.

(42) Reds shortstop in 1870 played in 52 games with a batting average of .518, 59 homeruns, and scored 339 runs.

(43) Cubs player/manager Cap Anson hated African Americans so much he was the influence in getting them banned from playing. He went to play a game in one city that featured a black catcher. Anson told the opposing team, "If the nigger plays, we don't."

(44) Ty Cobb was respected as a player, feared as a baserunner, and HATED by opposing players, fans, and even teammates.

(45) Cobb was violent and paranoid. He once went into the stands to attack a heckler, even though the man was disabled. The man had only part of one hand. When Cobb heard that he replied, "I don't care if he has no feet!" and continued to punch, kick and stomp the man.

(46) Cobb's biggest fear was getting hit by a Walter Johnson fastball.

(47) Cobb insulted everyone he could. Once he was riding Chief Yellow Horse while he was pitching, Cobb called him blanket ass, lousy Injun, etc. When Cobb went to bat bat Yellow Horse, who was known for his fastball and great control, beaned Cobb in the head. Cobb was carried off the field and taken to the hospital.

(48) Honus Wagner was cheerful and kind Shoeless Joe Jackson was charming, yet illiterate Christy Mathewson was intelligent, handsome, and college educated

(49) After Ray Chapman died from a beaning by Carl Mays, the spitball, dirty ball, and stained ball were all banned. Mays used all three.

(50) Hall Of Fame catcher Mickey Cochran was a master trash talker. When he was beaned late in his career, he spent several days in a coma. He never batted again.

(51) Burleigh Grimes was the last "legal" spitball pitcher.

(52) In 1930 the entire National League batted .303

(53) In the original rules of baseball it took 9 balls to be issued a base on balls.

(54) In 1922 Cobb batted .401 and didn't win a batting title! George Sisler batted .420

(55) Lefty Grove won 300 games in his career, but when he lost a game, even his team-mates avoided him.

(56) Babe Ruth was a publicity hound while Lou Gehrig was quiet and reserved.

(57) Rogers Hornsby made enemies in every town he played in.

(58) With the outbreak of World War II, baseball owners considered closing down the game, but President Roosevelt wrote the Commissioner and told him America needs baseball for moral support.

(59) Lou Gehrig drove in 174 runs in one year, but came in second in RBI's behind Hack Wilson who had 191.

(60) Braves Hall Of Fame third baseman Eddie Matthews turned down scholarships to play football at USC, UCLA, Stanford, and many more.

(61) Roger Maris rode the train to Norman, Oklahoma where he was to be met by an official from the University of Oklahoma and see about being signed to play football for the Sooners. No one showed, so after a few hours of waiting he got on another train and returned home. There he signed a baseball contract.

(62) Willie McCovey's first hit was a single off of Hall Of Famer Robin Roberts. He had three more singles that day.

(63) Juan Marichal was the first Latin American player inducted into the Baseball Hall of Fame.

(64) August 22, 1965, Marichal and Dodger catcher John Roseboro got into a confrontation at home plate and Marichal struck Roseboro in the head with his bat. He was ejected from the game, suspended for 9 games, and fined $1,750 by the league.

(65) In the early days of baseball up till the 1960's, it was considered a sign of luck to to find a hair pin. It meant you were going to get a hit in your next game.

(66) Joe Morgan, while playing second base for the Big Red Machine, became the first second bagger to win to win back-to-back MVP awards

(67) Hal Newhouser, Brooklyn Dodgers, was the first pitcher to win back-to-back MVP's

(68) California Angels pitcher Dean Chance was the youngest man to win the Cy Young Award at 23.

(69) Ferguson Jenkins threw 267 complete games in his career

(70) The 1949 batting race came down to fractions as George Kell batted .3429 and Ted Williams hit .3428

(71) When Harmon Killebrew retired he had hit at least 2 homeruns in every MLB park

(72) When Killebrew retired, no right handed batter had hit as many homeruns, 573, as he did. In a double header he hit 4 homeruns in the two games, still the only player to do so. He was nicknamed "Killer" because he literally killed the baseball, other than that he was one of the most popular and friendliest players ever.

(73) Pirate Ralph Kiner led the N.L. in homeruns 7 consecutive years.

(74) Sandy Koufax attended University of Cincinnati on a basketball scholarship.

(75) Gene Conley is the only person to play on a MLB championship team and a NBA championship team

(76) Chuck Connors, the actor better known as the RIFLEMAN played MLB for the Cubs and Dodgers. He, too, played in the NBA. He was the first person to shatter a back-board in a NBA game.

(77) In his first 6 years as a Dodger, Koufax was 36 – 40, but in 1961 when he learned how to control his fastball he was 129 – 47 in his next 6 years streak

(78) Cornelius McGillicuddy coached the Athletics for 50 years. Haven't heard of him?

Probably because he shortened his name so it would fit on a box score. Better known As Connie Mack

(79) Ferguson Jenkins is the only pitcher with 3000 strike outs and less than 1000 walks.

(80) The Homestead Grays of the Negro League won that title from 1937 to 1945.

Buck Leonard and Josh Gibson were their top players and team leaders.

(81) Rabbit Maranville once slid between the legs of umpire Hank O'Days legs while stealing a base.

(82) The Yankees won the A.L. pennant from 1949 to 1954 when the Indians broke their streak under manager Al Lopez. They then proceeded to win four more pennants before the White Sox won the A.L. pennant in 1959 under manager Al Lopez.

(83) In the 1960's, Juan Marichal was 24 – 1 at Candlestick Park.

(84) Burt Blyleven won 287 games as a MLB pitcher and was the first person from the Netherlands to play MLB.

(85) The first Native American to play MLB was Francis Sockalexis. The Cleveland Spiders changed their name to Indians to honor him.

(86) Dennis Martinez was from Nicaragua, won 245 games, and on July 28, 1991 became the oldest man to throw a perfect game.

(87) The first Canadian inducted into Cooperstown was Ferguson Jenkins.

(88) The first foreign born player enshrined into Cooperstown was Dominican born Roberto Clemente

(89) The youngest player elected to the Hall of Fame was Sandy Koufax.

(90) The first Jewish player enshrined in Cooperstown was Hank Greenberg.

He was the first MLB player to sign up when war was declared in 1941.

(91) The first Native American placed in the Hall was Chief Bender

(92) Despite breaking Babe Ruth's record of 60 homeruns in 1961, Roger Maris won back-to-back MVP awards in 1960 – 1961, won a Gold Glove, played in the All-Star game, and played in the World Series as a Yankee and a Cardinal. He still is not in the Hall-of-Fame.

(93) Hank Aaron hit 20 or more homeruns in 20 consecutive years.

(94) Aaron never won a homerun title

(95) In 1902 brothers Jack and Mike O'Neill became the first brother battery (that's pitcher/catcher) in MLB

(96) The first player to bat .300, hit 30 homers, drive in 100 runs, and steal 30+ bases in one season was Barry Bonds

(97) In 1927 Lloyd Waner, of the Pirates, won the batting title over his teammate and brother Paul. The first time brothers ever finished 1 and 2 in that category.

(98)   The first father/son combo to hit back-to-back homeruns in the same game was Ken Griffey Sr and Ken Griffey Jr

(99)   In 1992 when Fred McGriff won the homerun title, he became the first man to lead the N.L. one year and the A.L. another year.

BASEBALL VERSES ROUNDERS

Baseball truly is copied after a British playground game called ROUNDERS and here's how:

Rounders		Baseball
1.	a pitcher throws a ball	a pitcher throws a ball
2.	a striker hits the ball	a batter bats the ball
3.	has 4 stones or posts placed in a diamond shape	has four bases placed in a diamond shape

FIRST BLACK PLAYERS
FOR EACH TEAM

1. Dodgers, Jackie Robinson,   April 15, 1947
2. Indians, Larry Doby,   July 5, 1947
3. Browns, Hank Thompson,   July 17, 1947 (Browns are now the Orioles)
4. Giants, Monte Irvan,   July 8, 1949
5. Braves, Sam Jethroe,   April 18, 1950
6. White Sox, Minnie Minoso,   May 1, 1951
7. Athletics, Bob Trice,   September 13, 1953
8. Cubs, Ernie Banks,   September 17, 1953
9. Pirates, Curt Roberts,   April 13, 1954
10. Cardinals, Tom Alston,   April 13, 1954
11. Reds, Nino Esalera and Chuck Harmon,   April 17, 1954
12. Senators, Carlos Paula,   September 6, 1954 (now the Twins)
13. Yankees, Elston Howard,   April 14, 1955
14. Phillies, John Kennedy,   April 22, 1957
15. Tigers, Ozzie Virgil,   June 6, 1958
16. Red Sox, Pumpsie Green,   July 21, 1959

FATHER / SON PLAYERS IN MLB

1. Tim Raines (Rock) Sr and Tim Raines Jr......they appeared in 4 games together

2. Sandy Alomar Sr and Sandy Alomar Jr and Roberto.....both boys played for their dad with the Padres. Between the 3 there were 19 All-Star games, 11 Gold Gloves, 1 Rookie-of-the-Year, I Hall-of-Famer (Roberto)

3. Jose Cruz Sr and Jose Cruz Jr...................both played for the Astros

4. Tony Gwynn Sr and Tony Gwynn Jr.........both played for the Padres. Senior won 8 batting titles and was elected to the Hall-of-Fame

5. Felipe Alou and Moises Alou.......father coached son while with the Expos

6. Ray Boone and Bob Boone first family with 3 generations to the All-Star game

7. Bob Boone and Brett and Aaron Boone

8. Gus Bell and Buddy Bell

9.   Buddy Bell and David and Mike Bell

10.   Ken Griffey Sr and Ken Griffey Jr ……….both won All Star MVP awards, Junior is in Cooperstown

11.   Eddie Collins Sr and Eddie Collins Jr……Senior is the all-time leader for sacrifice hits in MLB

12.   Bobby Bonds Sr and Barry and Bobby Bond Jr……between Senior and Barry there was 11 Gold Gloves, 14 All Star games, and a MLB (for father/sons) record 1,094 homeruns

13.   Sammy Hairston and Jerry Hairston

14.   Jerry Hairston and Jerry Hairston Jr, Johnny, and Scott

15.   Ducky Schofield and Dick Schofield…..Dick's sister was married to Dennis Werth who has a step-son Jayson Werth

16.   Joe Coleman Sr and Joe Coleman Jr and Casey

17.   Ed Runge and Paul and Brian Runge (all 3 MLB umpires)

18.   Famed Cub announcer Harry Caray has two sons, Skip and Chip, that are also announcers

19.   Shag Crawford (an umpire) has two sons, one, Jerry is an ump and Joe is a NBA referee

20.   Reggie Jackson's father Martinez was a star in the Negro Leagues

21. Besides having a son playing baseball, Felipe Alou has two brothers, Matty and Jesus. All three started with the Giants and in one game all three started in the outfield on the same day, a MLB first

22. Cecil and son, Prince, are the only father/son to hit 50 homers in a year. Cecil retired with 319 career homers and Prince retired with? 319

23. Darrell Miller played in the MLB, brother Reggie Miller in the NBA, and sister Cheryl Miller played in the WNBA.

24. Gary Sheffield is Dwight Gooden's nephew

25. Shane Monahan's grandfather and great grandfather are members of the NHL Hall of Fame

26. Mel Rojas Sr has a son, Mel Rojas Jr, in MLB

27. Mel Rojas Sr is the nephew of the Alou brothers

28. Dave Magaden, former Mets coach, is Lou Piniella's cousin

29. J.T. Snow's father is former L.A. Rams wide receiver Jack Snow

30. Reggie Jackson is a cousin-in-law of Bobby Bonds

31. Tony Gwynn also had a brother in the MLB, Chis Gwynn

32. Dave Duncan, considered to be one of the best pitching coaches of all time, had two sons to play MLB, Chris and Shelley

33. The three Alou brothers wasn't the only trio of brothers in MLB. There were the Drew brothers (J.D., Tim, and Stephen) and the Molina trio of catchers (Bengie, Izzy, and Yadier).

34. Let's not forget the DiMaggio's (Dom, Vince, and, of course Hall of Famer Joe)

35. Joe, Luke and Tommie Sewell all three appeared in MLB. Joe is in Cooperstown

36. Hall of Famer Vladimar Guerro had a brother, Wilton, to play with him with the Expos

37. There was also Tommie and Willie Davis

38. Hall of Famer Pedro Martinez also played with his brother Ramon while with the Dodgers

39. Hall member Greg Maddux had brother Mike playing MLB

40. The Sadowski brothers, Bob, Ed, and Ted played in the majors
    As did the Mansell's, John, Mike, and Tom

41. The Sowders, Bill, John, and Len
    Jack, Jim, Mike, and Steve O'Neill
    John, Tom, and Jim Paciorek
    George, Harry, and Sam Wright
    Pascual, Melido, and Carlos Perez

42. Then the DeLahanty brothers: Ed (a Hall of Fame member) Frank, Jim, Joe, and Tom

43. Sandy Koufax was married to actor Richard Widmark's daughter

44. Ray Knight was married to LPGA Champion Nancy Lopez

45. Former Dodger Steve Yeager is record setting jet pilot Chuck Yeager's nephew

46. Former MLB reliever great Tug McGraw is the father of country singer/actor Tim McGraw

47. Joe DiMaggio was married to Marilyn Monroe

48. Kate Upton is also known as Mrs. Justin Verlander

49. Actress/Model Joanna Garcia is wed to Nick Swisher

50. Oklahoma State All-American softball pitcher is married to Jason Bay

51. All-American Jennie Finch's husband is Casey Daigle

52. Former MLB player David Justice was married to Halle Berry

53. Former major leaguer Pete Lacock's aunt was actress Joanne Dru and his father was actor/singer/star of Hollywood Squares Peter Marshall

54. Actress Chelsea Courtney is the daughter of Pete Rose

55. Leo Durocher was married to actress Laraine Day

56. Former Red Sox star Nomar Garciaparra was married to U.S. Womens Soccer Star Mia Hamm

57. R&B singer Anisha Nicole is Tony Gwynn Sr's daughter

58. Tennis Legend Billie Jean King's brother is Randy Moffitt, former MLB player

59. Lefty Gomez was married to Broadway actress June O'Dea

60. Tom Brady is baseballer Kevin Youkilis' brother in law

THEY SAID WHAT?

The Mighty Casey loved to talk and had some good lines such as:

After being released by the Yankees after WINNING the World Series for, what they called a "youth movement" he told the press, "If you like your job, don't ever turn 70."

In 1962 while coaching the pathetic Mets he commented, "Can anyone on this team play this game?"

He told one reporter, "These guys have found ways to lose that I've never seen before and I've been around this game for 100 years."

He had one player, Joe Christopher, that spoke Spanish to teach aging outfielder Richie Ashburn how to say "I've got it!" in Spanish so he and Elio Chaco wouldn't crash into each other on fly balls to short leftfield. Ashburn learned how to say "Yo La Tengo!"

Then big brawny Frank Thomas, playing centerfield, crashed into the aging Ashburn on a fly ball Ashburn had called Chaco off of. To which Casey said, "With this team you can get hurt no matter what language you speak."

The poor Mets won only 20 games all year, out of 160. Their longest winning streak was 3 games. There were two pitchers named Bob Miller, so Casey called on Miller and the other Nelson.

HERE IS A COLLECTION OF SOME MORE OF HIS QUOTES

"All right everyone, line up in alphabetically order according to your height."

"Never make predictions, especially about the future."

"Being with a woman never hurt no professional ballplayer. It's staying up all night looking for one a woman that does him in."

"The trick is growing up without getting old."

"Without losers where would the winners be?"

"I got players with bad watches, they can't tell midnight from noon."

"When you are younger you get blamed for crimes you never committed and when you're older you begin to get credit for virtues you never possessed. It evens out."

"Good pitching will always beat good hitting and vise-versa."

To a player that had been released, "Son, we'd like to keep you around this season, but we're going to try and win a pennant."

When Mickey Mantle asked him if he ever played baseball, "Sure I played, did you think I was born at the age of seventy sitting in a dugout trying to manage guys like you?"

"There comes a time in every man's life and I've had plenty of them."

"Managing is a job where you get paid for homeruns that someone else hits."

AND THEN THERE'S YOGISM

"If you don't know where you are going, you might wind up someplace else."

To a group of reporters, "If you ask me anything I don't know, I'm not going to answer."

"Baseball is 90 percent mental. The other half is physical."

"In theory there is no difference between theory and practice. In practice there is."

"You can observe a lot just by watching."

"The future ain't what it used to be."

"Half the lies they tell about me aren't true."

"I never said most of those things I said."

"It ain't over till it's over."

"When you come to the fork in the road, take it."

OTHER PLAYER'S AND COACHES HAD THEIR MOMENTS

"I never threw an illegal pitch. The trouble is once in a while I toss one that ain't never been seen by this generation." Satchel Paige

"Bob Gibson is the luckiest pitcher I have ever saw. He always pitches when the other team doesn't score any runs." Tim McCarver

"It took me 17 years to get 3000 hits in baseball, and I did it in one afternoon on the golf course." Hank Aaron

Dick Allen's opinion on artificial turf, "If a horse won't eat it, I don't want to play on it."

"There ain't much to being a ballplayer, if you're a ballplayer." Honus Wagner

"There are two theories on hitting the knuckleball, unfortunately neither one works." Charlie Lau, batting instructor

"The best way to catch a knuckleball is to wait for it to stop rolling and pick it up." Bob "Mr. Baseball" Ueker

"Slump? I ain't in no slump! I just ain't hitting nothing." Yogi Berra

"If you don't succeed at first. Try pitching." Jack Harshman

"The Yankees don't pay me to win everyday – just two out of three." The Old Perfessor aka Casey Stengal

"The key to winning baseball is pitching, fundamentals, and three run homers." Earl Weaver

"You can sum up the game in in one word: 'You never know'." Joaquin Andujar

"I went through my baseball career as the player to be named later." Joe Garagiola

"Orioles pitcher comes off the mound like a drunk kangaroo on roller skates." Joe Garagiola

Dizzy Dean to a batter, "Son, which kind of pitch would you like to miss?"

Garagiola was a great announcer, but, like his best friend, growing up in St Louis, Yogi Berra, had some ways to slip up what he meant to say. Such as. "Nolan Ryan's curve has been straightened out, making him a better pitcher."

"Baseball is like driving, it's the one who gets home safely that counts." Tommy Lasorda

"There are three types of players. (1) Those who make things happen, (2) those who watch it happen, and (3) those who wonder what the hell happened." Tommy Lasorda

"I knew my playing career was over when my baseball card came out with no picture." Bob Uecker

Umpires could also take the humor route:

Al Barlick told Leo "the Lip" Durocher one day, "We have another game here tomorrow night and either you or I are going to be absent." Durocher was suspended for 5 games.

Durocher could really get the umps dander up. Jocko Conlan told him one time, "Take a punch at me so I can knock your block off!"

The organist at the Reds' stadium insisted on playing while the game was being played. Jocko sent a message telling the organist to play between innings or "shut the hell up."

He was asked if there was a league rule about this. His answer, "Hell yes, I just made it."

Yogi Berra kept complaining about balls and strikes in one game so umpire Cal Hubbard finally said, "There is no sense in both of us calling this game. Since I'm getting paid to, and you're not, one of us has to go, and that will be you."

MORE FROM THE UKE

"I set records that will never be equaled in fact, I hope 90% of them ever get printed."

"Sporting good companies pay me NOT to endorse their products."

"Anybody with ability can play in the big leagues, but to be able to trick people year in and year out the way I did, I think is was a much greater feat."

"The fans in Philadelphia were tough. Opposing players and Phillies players really got abused. Once they had an Easter Egg hunt for all the little kids at the game. The fans BOOED the kids that couldn't find any."

While with the Cardinals, Hecker and Bob Gibson were fined one year after the team photo was shot, but before it was printed, when someone noticed the two of them were holding hands during the shot. Management was not happy, because they had to get all the people back together to re-do the shot.

"They broke it in gently they'd traded me. The manager came up to me and told me they didn't allow visitors in the clubhouse."

In one World Series before the game a jazz band was playing on the field. They went to take a break and Uke picked up the tuba and started shagging flies in the outfield. By the time the band came back the tuba was heavily damaged. He had to pay the tuba player $500 to replace his instrument and the N.L. fined him another 500.

Lefty Gomez told Lou Gehrig, "Hell, it took 15 years to get you out of the game, sometimes I don't last 15 minutes."

Gomez told the press one day, "I have a new invention. A revolving goldfish bowl, less work on the fish."

"How old would you be if you didn't know how old you were?" Satchel Paige

BASEBALL NICKNAMES

Charles "Chief" Bender

Bill "Moose" Skowron

Harold "Little Poison" Waner

Harold "Pie" Traynor

Edward "Whitey" Ford

Harry "The Cat" Brecheen

Elwin "Preacher" Roe

Don "Popeye" Zimmer

Phil "Scooter" Rizzuto

Orestes "Minnie" Minosa

Stan "the Man" Musial

John "Boog" Powell

Dave "Kong" Kingman

Paul "Big Poison" Waner

Willie "Say Hey" Mays

Lewis "Hack" Wilson

James "Cool Papa" Bell

Sal "The Barber" Maglie

Harold "Pee Wee" Reese

Leroy "Satchel" Paige

Enos "Country" Slaughter

"Sudden" Sam McDowell

Ewell "the Whip" Blackwell

Orlando "Baby Bull" Cepeda

Sam "Wahoo" Crawford

James "Dusty" Rhodes

Lawrence "Yogi" Berra

"Mr. Cub" Ernie Banks

Paul "Dazzy" Dean

Jim "Kitty" Kaat

Jim "Mudcat" Grant

Jimmy "Double X" Foxx

Jim "Catfish" Hunter

Tom "Terrific" Seaver

Denton "Cy" Young

"Rapid" Robert Feller

Harvey "the Kitten" Haddix

"Hammering" Hank Aaron

Mariano "Mo" Rivera

"Big Papi" David Ortez

Carlton "Pudge" Fisk

Willie "Pops" Stargell

Dave "Cobra" Parker

David "Boomer" Wells

Tony "El Gato" Pena

Mike "Human Rain Delay" Hargrove

Mitch "Wild Thing" Williams

Ryan "Hebrew Hammer" Braun

"Doctor Strange Glove" Dick Stuart

Julian "Phantom" Javier

Honus "Flying Dutchman" Wagner

Leo "the Lip" Durocher

Ted "Splendid Splinter" Williams

Juan "Gone" Gonzalez

Bob "Gibby" Gibson

Nolan "the Express" Ryan

Tom "Flash" Gordan

Greg "Mad Dog" Maddux

Calvin "Pokey" Reese

Hideki "Godzilla" Matsui

Steve "Rainbow" Trout

Will "The Thrill" Clark

Virgil "Fire" Trucks

George "Storm" Davis

Larry "Chipper" Jones

"Neon" Dion Sanders

Don "Big D" Drysdale

Charlie "Chili" Davis

Ron "Penguin" Cey

John "Pepper" Martin

Jim "Emu" Kern

Johnny "Boy General" Bench

Covelli "Coco" Crisp

"The Yankee Clipper" Joe DiMaggio

"Dominican Dandy" Juan Marichal

"Sweet" Lou Whitaker

"Wild Horse of the Osage" Pepper Martin

Rube "Black Snake" Currie	William "Judy" Johnson	Ralph "Spec" Bebop
George "Mule" Settles	Frank "Red Ant" Wickware	Jim "Mr. Ed" Bibby
"Big Dago" Joe DiMaggio	"Little Dago" Billy Martin	Wilbur "Bullet" Rogan
Johnnie "Dusty" Baker	Eddie "the Brat" Stankey	Louis "Top" Santop
Floyd "Jelly" Fowler	Carl "Yaz" Yazstrazemski	Devon "Devo" White
Paul "Motormouth" Blair	Ralph "Road Runner" Garr	Kent "Bones" Tekulve
Maury "Mousy" Wills	William "Gates" Brown	Johnny "Crab" Evers
Jim "Toy Cannon" Wynn	Craig "Pig Pen" Biggio	Daniel "Rusty" Staub
"King" Carl Hubbell	Carl "the Meal Ticket" Hubbell	Jim "Gumby" Gantner
Walter "Barney" Johnson	Walter "Big Train" Johnson	Lou "Biscuit Pants" Gehrig

ANOTHER "100" LIST

1. Baseball's first 200 career game winner was Albert Spaulding

2. The World's largest baseball collection can be found at the Metropolitan Museum of Art in New York City

3. The first player to appear in the Little League World Series and then in the MLB World Series was Oriole slugger Boog Powell

4. A 1987 winner of the New York Lottery used the numbers of his favorite baseball players

5. In 1997 the Orioles spent EVERY day of the season in 1st place

6. In 1918 the Red Sox won their 3rd world series in 4 years and would not win another until 2004

7. In 1949 Red Sox pitchers Ellis Kinder and Mel Parnell won 48 games between themselves. The rest of the team won 48 games combined.

8. From 1940 through 1949, Ted Williams hit more homeruns than anyone else, despite missing 1943 – 45 while serving as a fighter pilot in World War II

9. On opening day of 1944, Tuffy Rhodes smacked 3 homeruns for the Cubs, they still lost 12-8

10. In the entire 1950 season the White Sox had 19 stolen bases and in 1951 they had 93, and would start an eleven year stranglehold on the stolen base title

11. After 88 years the White Sox won it all in 2005

12. J.L Wilkinson, from Iowa, organized a team he called the All Nations Team. It consisted of all the things Ty Cobb hated, whites, blacks, Indians, Latinos, Asians, Cubans and a woman at 2B. They later moved from Des Moines to Kansas City in 1915

13. 27 Hall of Famers served in World War I
    36 in World War II
    6 in Korea

14. Larry McPhail served in WWI and WWII

15. Ted Williams served in WWII and Korea

16. Al Bumbry was a lieutenant and platoon leader in Viet Nam. He was also awarded the Bronze Star

17. Bobby Jones lost most of his hearing from artillery fire in Viet Nam

18. Carlos May lost part of his thumb by a mortar during Viet Nam

19. Harry O'Neil, Elmer Green, and Eddie Grant were the only MLB players to die in WWII

20. Bob Neighbors died in Korea, the only MLB player to do so

21. Despite winning the A.L. MVP in 1960 and 1961 and hitting 61 homeruns in 1960, the Yankee fans booed him unmercifully. In 12 years he played for the Indians, Athletics, Yankees, and Cardinals, played in 7 World Series, 7 All-Star Games, 1 Gold Glove, 2 A.L. RBI titles, 1 Runs scored title, 1 Homerun Title. He won 3 World Series rings, 2 as a Yankee (1961 and 1962) and 1 as a Cardinal (1967).

22. It was said that Oriole great Brooks Robinson could field a ball with a pair of plyers

23. On May 7, 1957, Vic Power hit a leadoff homerun and then in the 10th inning smashed a walk off homerun

24. Hall of Famer Joe Sewell batted 7,132 times in his MLB career and struck out 113 times. That figures to 1 strike out for every 63 at bats

25. In 1925 the Worcester, Massachusetts team had a terrible year. The General Manager released outfielder Casey Stengal, then fired manager Casey Stengal, then General Manager Casey Stengal resigned

26. Richie Ashburn was playing for the Phillies when Warren Spahn won his 100th career game. When Spahn won number 200 Ashburn was still with the Phillies, but when Spahn won number 300 against the Mets, Ashburn was playing for the Mets

27. Tom Seaver struck out 200 or more batters 9 consecutive years

28. Bill Veek, Jr planted the ivy in Wrigley Stadium when his father was General Manager for the Cubs

29. When Veek, Jr owned the Indians, he played the first black player in the A.L.

30. In 1941 on the last day of the season, Red Sox management told Ted Williams to set out due to the fact his batting average was .400 and he could hold that average by not playing. Williams refused and played anyhow. In the doubleheader Williams went 4 for 6 and finished his season at .406

31. In one of his last seasons, Ted Williams demanded a contract talk. He wanted to take a CUT in pay, because he had such a bad year before. When management refused, he sat out the start of the season for two weeks when management gave in to his demands.

32. Ted Williams, Teddy Ballgame, the Splendid Splinter was a true baseball fan. On his very last at bat of his distinguished career, Ted Williams HOMERED

33. Lloyd and Paul Waner played the outfield for the Pirates for 14 years, together

34. Warren Spahn was born in 1921
    Made his MLB debut when he was 21
    Wore the number 21 and 7 times he won 21 games

35. No two teammates have hit as many homeruns as has Hank Aaron and Eddie Mathews

36. Tom Glavine was drafted in the NHL draft

37. Kenny Loftin was starting guard for Arizona

38. Dave Lopes set a MLB record by becoming the oldest man to steal 20 or more bases when he was 40

39. Hack Wilson stood 5'6" tall, weighed around 200 pounds, had an 18" neck, a big stomach, and wore size 6 shoes

40. Jim DeShais, of the Astros, on September 23, 1986, struck out the first 8 batters he faced, establishing a MLB mark

41. Ruben Sierra, a Ranger, smacked two homeruns in a game, one from each side of the plate, at the age of 20

42. Shoeless Joe Jackson batted .400 or better 3 times and never won a batting title, including his rookie season when he batted .408

43. Bill Wambsganss pulled off an unassisted triple play in a World Series game

44. The only player to be a MLB All-Star and NFL Pro Bowler in the same year was Bo Jackson

45. The only player to play in a World Series and Superbowl the same year was Dieon Sanders

46. John Lynch threw the first pitch for the Marlins very first game. He then appeared in 9 Pro Bowls

47. Kenny Loftin played in 2 NCAA Final Fours and 2 MLB World Series, the only one to achieve that

48. Tom Glavin was drafted in the NHL draft ahead of hockey Hall of Famers Brett Hull and Luv Robitaille

49. Dave DeBusschere threw a shut out for the White Sox, played with the NBA Champion Knicks, and was elected as a U.S. Senator

50. Jackie Jensen is the only player to play in the Rose Bowl and win the MVP in baseball

51. Chuck Conners was a NBA backup for the Celtics

52. Tony Gwynn was a 3rd round draft pick of the Padres and a 10th round pick in the NBA

53. Dave Winfield was drafted by the MLB, NBA, ABA, and NFL

54. Brian Jordan, Drew Henson, D.J. Dozier, and Tim Tebow all played in the NFL and MLB

55. Bob Gibson played briefly with the Globetrotters

56. The first team to win 100 games in only their second year in existence was the Diamondbacks

57. In 1979, Braves knuckleballer Phil Niekro led the N.L. with 21 wins and he also led the N.L. with 20 losses. His 21 wins was a tie with Astro knuckleballer Joe Niekro

58. Braves John Smoltz recorded a decision in three different decades in 3 All-Star games. He lost in 89, won in 96, and lost in 05.

59. The 1971 Orioles had 4 twenty game winning pitchers, Dave McNally 21, Jim Palmer 20, Pat Dobson 20, and Mike Cuellar 20.

60. The Yankees set a MLB homerun record 241 as a team in 1961. That record would stand until 1996 when the Orioles smashed 257

61. 1971 Tiger relief ace, John Hiller, suffered a stroke. In 1973 he had 38 saves, a record then, and won Fireman-of-the-Year and Comeback Player of the year

62. In 1997 Charles Johnson set a MLB mark for a catcher by handling 973 chances in 123 games without and error

63. April 15, 1968 the Astros beat the Mets 1-0 in twenty four innings

64. In 1979Catcher Darrell Porter became the 2nd catcher in A.L. history to collect 100 runs scored, 100 RBIs, and 100 walks in a season. Mickey Cochran was the first.

65. In 1964 the Angels threw 28 shutouts, 11 by Dean Chance

66. In 1973 Nolan Ryan won 21 games, pitched 26 complete games, struck out 367 batters, and fanned 19 in a game 3 times

67. Babe Ruth copied his batting swing from Shoeless Joe

68. Joe Jackson called his bat Black Betsy. It weighed 48 ounces

69. Ruth's bat weighed 52 ounces

70. Besides playing and coaching, Bobby Valentine also had restaurants, where he invented sandwich wraps

71. Mickey Mantle's number 7 was retired, but when he first came up he wore #6

72. When MLB retired number 42 in 1997 only players wearing that number before that year could wear it

73. The Yankees added their numbers on their jerseys they went by where they batted in the order, thus Ruth, who batted 3rd wore #3

74. In 1988 the very last player drafted was Mike Piazza

75. Nolan Ryan pitched in 4 decades, (69, 70, 80, and 90's)

76. Ryan pitched for 27 years, threw 7 no-hitters, was the oldest man to throw a no-hitter, and oldest man to strike out 300 batters

77. The oldest man to appear in an All-Star Game was Satchel Paige

78. The youngest pitcher to ever start an All-Star game was Jerry Walker, at age of 20, he is also the youngest man to win an All-Star Game

79. In 1965 when Paige was 59, Bill Veek Jr signed him to pitch one game. He did, 3 shutout innings

80. The oldest position player in MLB was Julio Franco at the age of 48

81. The oldest pitcher to record a win was Jamie Moyer on May 16, 2012

82. The oldest player to record an RBI in a game was Jamie Moyer on May 16,2012

83. In 2004 Jose Bautista played for 4 different teams

84. On August 4, 1982, Met Joel Youngblood got a hit. In between the twinbill, Youngblood was traded to the Expos. He got to Montreal in time to go in and bat in the 8th inning he was sent in to pinch hit and he got a hit. He is the only player to get a hit for two different teams in two different games in two different cities on the same day

85. In 2012 Octavio Dotel joined his 13th major league team

86. The record for most consecutive scoreless innings in the World Series is Babe Ruth, with 29

87. In 45 play-off and World Series games only 2 out of 45 baserunners succeeded in stealing off of Johnny Bench

88. After Joe DiMaggio's 56 game hitting streak ended he started a 17 game streak the next day

89. Dodger pitcher Don Drysdale hit 7 homeruns in one season

90. In his major league debut at 17 years old, Robert Feller struck out 15 batters

91. On September 8, 1965 Bert Campaneris of the Athletics, played all 9 positions in a game

92. Robert Feller would win 107 games before he was 23

93. Jose Altuve is the shortest player to ever win the MVP award.

94. Since he debuted in 2011, Altuve has won 1 MVP, 5 Silver Slugger Awards, 1 Gold Glove, 2 Player-of-the-Year awards, and a World Series ring

95. Mariano Rivera saved a MLB record 652 games

96. Most Innings pitched in a season with 376 2/3 is knuckleballer Wilbur Wood

97. Ichiro Suzuki had 200 or more hits for 10 straight years

98. Fernando Tatis hit 2 grand slams in one game, in the same inning

99. Stan Musial hit 177 career triples

100. Curtis Granderson hit 23 triples in one year

RECORDS CONSIDERED UNBREAKABLE

DEAD BAll ERA			LIVE BALL ERA
1.	Cy Young, 511	WINS IN A CAREER	Warren Spahn, 363
2.	Hoss Radbourn, 59	WINS IN SEASON	Dizzy Dean, 31
3.	Cy Young, 749	COMPLETE GAMES IN CAREER	Warren Spahn, 382
4.	Will White, 75	COMPLETE GAMES IN SEASON	Grover Cleveland Alexander, 33 Burleigh Grimes, 33 Dizzy Trout, 33
5.	George Bradley, 16	SHUTOUTS IN ONE SEASON	Bob Gibson, 13

6. Career shutouts is 110 held by Walter "Big Train" Johnson

7. Jack Taylor pitched 202 games from June 20, 1901 to August 13, 1906 without being relieved

8. Consecutive no-hitters, 2, Johnny Vander Meer (Max Scherzer tossed a 1 hitter and no hitter back-to-back in 2015)

9. Most career no-hitters, 7, Nolan Ryan (also the oldest man to throw a no-hitter)

10. Most career strikeouts, 5714, Nolan Ryan (also oldest man to strike out 300 in a season)

11. Most career walks, 2795, Nolan Ryan

12. Most Career Saves, 652, Mariano Rivera

13. Most Innings pitched in a season, 376 2/3, Wilbur Wood (with lack of pitchers throwing complete games, this could hold a long time)

14. Career hits, 4256, Pete Rose (that alone should be Hall-of-Fame recognition)

15. Hits in a season, 262, Ichiro Suzuki (when American born Randy Bass was on track to break the season homerun record in Japan, the Japanese pitched around him the last two games. Why didn't MLB do that to Ichiro?)

16. Consecutive years with 200 or more hits, 10, Ichiro

17. Career triples, 177, Stan Musial

18. Triples in a season, 23, Curtis Granderson

19. Most grand slams in one inning, 2, Fernando Tatis Sr

20. Live ball highest career batting average, .344, Ted Williams

21. Runs batted in in a season, 191, Hack Wilson

22. Highest on base percentage in a career, .482, Ted Williams

MAJOR LEAGUE PLAYERS FROM AROUND THE WORLD

On April 26, 2017 Mpho' Gift Ngoepe became the first player from continental Africa (South Africa) to appear in a major league baseball game. Following is a list of the first players from their country to make an appearance in a MLB game.

1. Canada...........................Bob Addy.............................. 1876

2. Germany.........................George Heubel..................... 1876

3. Australia ....Joe Quinn............................ 1884

4. Netherlands ....John Houseman.................. 1894

5. Columbia ....Luis Castro 1902

6. Cuba................................Rafael Almedia.................... 1911

7. Puerto Rico ....Hiram Bithorn 1942

8. Venezuela........................Chico Carrasquel 1950

9. Dominican Republic ....Ozzie Virgil........................... 1956

10. Panama...........................Humberto Robinson 1955

11. Virgin Islands....................Joe Christopher....................1959

12. Nicaragua.........................Dennis Martinez..................1976

13. Aruba................................Gene Kinsdale.....................1996

14. Taiwan..............................Chen Chin-Feng..................2002

15. Japan...............................Masanori Murakamis...........1964

16. Mexico..............................Baldomero Almeda..............1933

17. Brazil................................Yan Gomez.........................2012

18. Curacao............................Hensley Meulens................1989

19. Lithuania..........................Dovydas Neverauskas.........2017

20. Hong Kong........................Austin Robert Brice.............2016

DID YOU KNOW

Willie Mays debuted on May 25, 1951 and went 0 for 5 in his first game. He went on to go 0 for 24 and went to manager Leo Durocher and told him to send him back down to the minors. Durocher refused, Mays started hitting and he was named rookie-of-the-year.

Casey Stengal debuted on July 27, 1912 and was 4 of 4 at bat. Casey remarked, later, "I broke in 4-4 and the writers decided they had seen the new Ty Cobb. It only took a few days for them to correct that impression."

On May 30, 1922 during a break of a doubleheader, the Cardinals traded Cliff Heathcote to the Cubs for Max Flack. The two players walked across the field, exchanged dugouts, changed into new uniforms and continued to play the next game.

On June 26, 1924 the Braves sent Jesse Barnes to the mound against the Giants whose pitcher that day was Virgil BARNES, Jesse's brother. This was the first time in MLB history that brothers opposed each other on the mound.

If you saw The Natural, with Robert Redford, you may remember his character hitting a ball that shattered a clock. May 30, 1946 Bama Rowell actually did smash the Bolivia Clock at Ebbetts Field, thus the inspiration for the movie.

The first player in MLB to have his number retired was Lou Gehrig

Johnny Mize was the first player to hit two 3 run homers in a game

The first All-Star game was played on July 6, 1933

The first player to oppose the MLB draft and refuse to play for who drafted him was Chuck Conners

The first manager to be tossed out of both games of a doubleheader was Mel Ott

June 17, 1957 Richie Ashburn hit the same fan twice with foul balls in the same at bat

Wrigley Field is known as the friendly confines

In 1992 Chris Hoiles, while catching for the Orioles, had 20 homeruns and 40 runs batted in, a record

In three World Series Ty Cobb batted .262 and hit 0 homers

Joe Niekro hit only one homerun in his career and it was off of his brother Phil

The first man to hit a homerun and score a touchdown in the same week was Jim Thorpe

Satchel Paige's Hall-of-Fame record shows a win – loss record of 28-31, but in the Negro Leagues he won nearly 2000!!

Babe Ruth's pitching record was 94 – 46

Bing Crosby was once part owner of the Pirates

One cowhide will make 5 baseball gloves

In 1959 MLB passed a rule that all ballparks right and left fields HAVE to be at least 325' from homeplate

The Reds once sent an autographed 2nd base to one Leonard Sly because 2nd base was once the site of his boyhood home. In case you don't know who Mr. Sly was, he went by the name ROY ROGERS

MLB bats are made from ash trees

The first two homers hit in Yankee Stadium were hit by a New York Giant outfielder by the name of Casey Stengal

Ty Cobb had a brand of cigarette named after him

Honus Wagner sued a cigarette company for putting a likeness of him on the back of their product, and won

NFL Hall-of-Famer Ernie Nevers gave up two of Babe Ruth's 60 homers

Hank Aaron, Felipe Alou, and Phil Roof are the only players to play for the Milwaukee Braves and Milwaukee Brewers

Joe and Vince DiMaggio are the only brothers to hit homers in the same All-Star game

When Bobby Thompson hit "the shot heard around the world" in 1951, Willie Mays was the on deck batter

Shoeless Joe Jackson is the only rookie to bat .400

Stu Miller was charged with a balk in the 1961 All-Star game when the wind in Candlestick Park blew him off the rubber as he was getting ready to throw the ball to the catcher

In 1988 Tommy John committed 4 errors all year, but 3 were on the same day, same game, and same play

George Brett is the only batter to win batting titles in three decades (70's, 80's, and 90's)

When the Reds traded Pedro Borbon he reacted by placing a voodoo curse on the organization

Hall-of-Fame Announcer Red Barber announced his first game, for the Reds, in 1934, despite having NEVER watched a game in his life

In the 7th inning of the 1964 World Series, both, Ken Boyer (Cardinals) and Clete Boyer (Yankees) homered. Another first and only brother thing.

The average life span of a baseball in the majors is 5 pitches

Looking For A Place To Go On Vacation

1.   National Baseball Hall of Fame, Cooperstown, New York

2.   Field of Dreams movie set, Dyersville, Iowa

3.   Negro League Baseball Museum, Kansas City, Missouri

4. Little League International Complex, South Williamsport, Pennsylvania

5. Rockwood Field, oldest standing professional ballpark, site of movies Cobb and Soul of the Game, Birmingham, Alabama

6. The Green Monster, Boston, Massachusetts

7. Rosenblatt Stadium, site of the college World Series, Omaha, Nebraska

8. Dodgertown, Vero Beach, Florida

9. Wrigleyville, Chicago, Illinois

10. National Baseball of Congress Hall-of-Fame, Wichita, Kansas

11. Legends of the Game Museum, Arlington, Texas

12. Ted Williams Museum and Hitters Hall-of-Fame, St Petersburgh, Florida

13. Louisville Slugger Museum, Atlanta, Georgia

14. Braves Museum, Atlanta, Georgia

15. Cardinals Museum, St Louis, Missouri

16. Yogi Berra Museum, Little Falls, New York

17. Heroes of Baseball, Cooperstown, New York

18. Reds Hall-of-Fame, Cincinnati, Ohio

19. House of David Museum, Benton Harbor, Michigan

20. Nolan Ryan Center, Alvin, Texas

21. National College Hall-of-Fame, Lubbock, Texas

22. Mickey Mantle Memorial Exhibit, Grove, Oklahoma

23. AT&T Bricktown Ballpark, Oklahoma City, Oklahoma

24. AT&T Ballpark, San Francisco, California

25. Camden Yards, Baltimore, Maryland

26. Busch Stadium III, St Louis, Missouri

27. Dodger Stadium, Los Angeles, California

28. PNC Park, Pittsburgh, Pennsylvania

29. Coors Park, Denver, Colorado

30. Yankee Stadium, Bronx, New York

31. Petco Field, San Diego, California

32. CITI Field, Queens, New York

33. Safeco Field, Seattle, Washington

34. Kauffman Stadium, Kansas City, Missouri

35. Minute Maid Park, Houston, Texas

36. Globe Life Park, Arlington, Texas

37. Comerica Park, Detroit, Michigan

38. Target Field, Minneapolis, Minnesota Miller Park, Milwaukee, Wisconsin

39. Sun Trust Park, Atlanta, Georgia

40. Citizens Bank Park, Philadelphia, Pennsylvania

41. Progressive Field, Cleveland, Ohio

42. Rogers Centre, Toronto, Ontario

43. Great American Ball Park, Cincinnati, Ohio

44. Nationals Park, Washington D.C.

45. Marlins Park, Miami, Florida

46. Angel Stadium, Anaheim, California

47. Chase Field, Phoenix, Arizona

48. Guaranteed Rate Field, Chicago, Illinois

49. Oakland-Alameda County Coliseum, Oakland, California

50. Tropicana Field, St Petersburgh, Florida

51. Fifth Third Field, Toledo, Ohio

52. Coca-Cola Field, Buffalo, New York

53. Whataburger Field, Corpus Christi, Texas

54. Dell Diamond, Frisco, Texas

55. McCormick Field, Ashville, North Carolina

56. Chickasaw Bricktown Ballpark, Oklahoma City, Oklahoma

57. AutoZone Park, Memphis, Tennessee

58. Modern Woodmen Park, Davenport, Iowa

59. Louisville Slugger Park, Louisville, Kentucky

60. FirstEnergy Stadium, Reading, Pennsylvania

61. And of course Wrigley Field

MORE FAMOUS FIRSTS

April 14, 1993 with catcher Dave Nillson and pitcher Lloyd Graeme as the battery for the Brewers, was the first time fellow Australians formed battery in a game

Tony Oliva became the first rookie to win a batting title in the 20th century, in 1964

The first man to hit 3 homeruns in the Senators Griffith Stadium was Joe DiMaggio

In 1970 Bob Gibson shared the A.L. title for wins with Gaylord Perry and the N.L. wins leader was Jim Perry. The only time brothers led the league in wins in the same year

The first player to receive one million votes for the All-Star game was Rod Carew from the Twins, in 1977

Johan Santana, in 2004, became the 1st Venezuelan to win 20 games in a year

In 1977 when Joe Torre became manager of the Mets, it was the first time a native New Yorker had ever been named manager of any MLB New York City based team

The first man to hit a grand slam in both games of a doubleheader was Robin Ventura, from the White Sox, in 1999

The first switch hitter to win a batting title was Mickey Mantle

Yankee reliever Sparky Lyle was the first relief pitcher to win the A.L. Cy Young Award, in 1977

In 1963 Yankee backstop became the first African American to win the A.L. MVP award

The first sibling pitching/catching battery in the same game was Tommy (P) and Homer (C) Thompson in 1912

Babe Ruth was the 1st man to strike out 1000 times in a career in 1930

The 1st man to hit 4 homeruns in a game in the 20th Century was Lou Gehrig

In 1949, Joe DiMaggio became the 1st $100,000 player

The first pitcher to throw 2 no-hitters in a season was Yankee great, and Oklahoman Native American, Allie "Chief" Reynolds

In 1991 Dennis Eckersley became the first man with 150 wins as a starter and 150 saves as a reliever

Jose Canseco, in 1988, became the first man to hit 40 homers and steal 40 bases the same year

On August 5, 1921 the Pirates became the 1st MLB team to broadcast a game over the radio

The first time brothers were 1st and 2nd in the batting title race was 1927 when Lloyd Waner batted .380 and brother Paul .355 (a couple more Oklahoma boys)

October 13, 1971 the Pirates beat the Orioles 4-3 in the 1st World Series game played at night

In 1990, Barry Bonds became the first player to bat .300, hit 30 homers, drive in 100 runs, and steal 50 bases

In 1992 Fred McGriff became the first man to lead both leagues in homeruns in different seasons

On June 1, 1923 the Giants became the first team to score in every inning of a nine inning game

In 1990 the Mariners signed free agent Ken Griffey Sr, thus becoming the first team to have father and son playing on the same team. Later that year they became the first father/son combo to hit back-to-back homers in the same game

The Griffey's are the only father and son to have won the All-Star MVP award

In 1975, Fred Lynn became the first man to win the rookie-of-the-year and MVP the same year

Fred Lynn remains the only player to hit a grand slam in an All-Star game

The 1st Dominican player to win the MVP was George Bell in 1987

The 1st African American manager to lead his team to the play-offs was Cito Gaston

Tim Raines, in 1983, became the 1st player to steal 70 bases and have 70 RBIs

The first and only rookie to win 28 games was Grover Cleveland Alexander

Luke Appling was the 1st shortstop to get 3000 hits

The 1st catcher to catch with one hand was Johnny Bench

The 1st catcher to use the sweep tag was Johnny Bench

The 1st catcher to wear a helmet while batting was Johnny Bench

The MVP (Most Valuable Player) awards were not given until 1931. The 1st A.L. winner was Lefty Grove and the 1st N.L. winner was Frankie Frisch

The 1st All-Star game was played in Comiskey Park and won by the A.L. 4-2 behind Babe Ruth's two homeruns

In 1966 Frank Robinson, Orioles, won the Triple Crown Award in the A.L. and in 1967 Red Sox slugger Carl Yazstrezmski won the Triple Crown

Willie Mays was the 1st player to hit 30 homeruns and steal 30 bases in a year

1st player to hit 400 homeruns and steal 400 bases was Barry Bonds

1st man to hit 30 homers in a year was Babe Ruth

1st to hit 40 homers was Babe Ruth

1st to hit 50 homers was Babe Ruth

1st to hit 60 homers was Babe Ruth

1st to hit 70 homers was Mark McGwire

1st African American to homer in his first at bat was Dan Bankhead on August 26, 1947

1st black pitcher to face a black batter was Don Newcombe

1st black batter to face a black pitcher was Hank Thompson (an Okie)

September 1, 1971 the 1st ALL BLACK lineup was fielded by the Pirates

1st black pitcher to throw a no-hitter in MLB was Sam Jones on May 12, 1955

1st Grand slam in a World Series was on October 10, 1920 by Elmer Smith

1st brothers to play against each other in a World Series was Doc and Jimmy Johnson on October 6, 1920

Gene Conley is the only man to be on a World Series Championship team (1957, Braves) and NBA World Championship team (Celtics, 1959,1960, and 1961)

1ˢᵗ player to make $1 million a year was Nolan Ryan

1ˢᵗ team to draw 3,000,000 fans in a year was the Los Angeles Dodgers in 1978

1ˢᵗ player to win the Rookie-of-the-Year Award, Cy Young Award, and MVP in the same year was Don Newcombe in 1956

1ˢᵗ player to throw a no-hitter in his first major league start was Bobo Holloman on May 6, 1953

1ˢᵗ catcher to hit 2 grand slams in the same game was Chris Hoiles on August 14, 1998

1ˢᵗ pitcher to win World Series starts for 3 different teams was Curt Schilling (Phillies, Diamondbacks, and Red Sox)

1ˢᵗ man to win a batting title without playing a regular position was Billy Goodman in 1950 (45 games in the outfield, 27 at third base, 21 at first, 5 at second, and 1 at shortstop)

1ˢᵗ time rookie brothers started at pitcher against each other was on September 29, 1986 when the Cubs sent Greg Maddux to the mound against the Phillies, who sent Mike Maddux to pitch

1ˢᵗ player to have back-to-back 60 homerun years was Sammy Sosa in 1998 and 1999

1ˢᵗ Latin American player to play in the All-Star game was Chico Carrasquel in 1951

1ˢᵗ perfect game pitched in the 20ᵗʰ Century was thrown on April 20,

1922 by a rookie from the White Sox named Charlie Robertson, beating the Tigers 2-0

1st MVP player to wear glasses was Dick Allen in 1972

1st player to lead the A.L. in triples 4 years in a row was White Sox outfielder Lance Johnson

1st A.L. player to bat .300, hit 30 homeruns, and drive in 100 runs, hit 40 doubles, and steal 25 bases was White Sox Magglio Ordonez, in 2001

1st President to attend a MLB game was Benjamin Harrison on June 2, 1892 in a game between the Senators and Reds

1st night game was won by the Reds 2-1 over the Phillies on May 24, 1935

1st African American manager in MLB was Frank Robinson for the Indians in 1975

1st 20 game winning pitcher to wear glasses was Mel Harder in 1934

1st A.L. night game the Indians defeated the Athletics 8-3 in 10 innings on May 16, 1939

1st pitcher to throw an opening day no-hitter was Bob Feller on April 16, 1940 as the Indians defeated the White Sox 1-0

1st African American pitcher to throw a shut-out was Satchel Paige in 1948

1st African American to pitch in a World Series was Satchel Paige in 1948

1st expansion team player to win a batting title was Rockies Andres Galarraga in1993

1st team to hit 200 homeruns and steal 200 bases was the 1996 Rockie1st team to have 4 different players to hit 30 homeruns in a year was the 1996 Rockies and again in 1997

1st team to win the World Series in November was the 2001 Diamondbacks

1st team to win 100 games was the 1892 Boston Bean eaters

1st player to get 200 hits in both leagues was George Sisler

1st team to have 9 starters with 20 homeruns in a season was the 1996 Orioles

FOR YOUR INFORMATION

May 26, 1959, Pirates Harvey Haddix entered the 13th inning pitching a perfect game against the Braves. Felix Mantilla reached 1st base on and error, still got a no-hitter going, Mantilla is sacrificed to 2nd. Hank Aaron is intentionally walked and Joe Adcock follows with a three run homerun, BUT as Mantilla is scoring, Aaron walks to the dugout, thinking the game is a final, and Adcock rounding the bases is called out for passing Aaron. The homerun is declared a double. Still, Haddix lost, 1-0

Jerry Remy went to bat 2,292 times without hitting a homerun

Duane Kuipper went 1,997 at bats without a homerun

Al Newman went 1,893 at bats with no homerun

In 23 years as a pitcher, Don Sutton went 0-1354 on homeruns

On September 28, 1960 Ted Williams went to bat in the 8th inning for his final MLB at bat of his illustrious career and, on the third pitch, hit a homerun

May 25, 1937 Mickey Cochrane hit a game tying homerun in the 3rd inning off of Yankee pitcher Bump Hadley. Two innings later Cochrane was on the ground at home plate, his head fractured in three places. At 34, in his prime as a player and manager was finished. After spending a week in a coma he recovered, but never played again, though he would manage. Since a hit batter is not considered an at bat, officially, Cochrane's last hit was a homerun

October 6, 1906 Chick Stahl was completing his 10th year as a star. He was now acting manager for the Red Sox, whom he had helped win 4 pennants. On this day, with the score 5-2 in favor of the hated Yankees, he smashed a two run homerun on what would be his last at bat, as the Bo-Sox last 5-4. On March 28, 1907, at the age of 34, Chick Stahl committed suicide

Mike Cubbage hit only 34 homeruns in his career, but some of his shots were important. 4 came with the bases loaded, the first one being his 1st major league at bat in 1975. He hit one in 1976, 1977, and 1978. The 1975 grand slammer was part of a 5 RBIs he had in one inning. The 1978 slam was part of a cycle he hit for. On October 3, 1981 in his last at bat he hit a solo shot to end his career.

Joe Rudi is the only batter to homer in his last at bat in a regular season and his last at bat in a World Series

September 30, 1984 Padre Eddie Miller hit a solo homerun that was his final at bat and his ONLY homerun of his career

In 1973 the Braves had 3 batters hit 40 or more homeruns (Dave Johnson 43, Darrell Evans 41, and Hank Aaron 40)

Hank Aaron never won a homerun title

Tony Conigliaro of the Red Sox was the fastest batter to 100 career homers than anyone. He was 25. Then he was beaned by Yankee pitcher Jack Hamilton, virtually ending his career

The youngest player to hit a MLB homer was Tommy Brown at age 17

The oldest to hit a homer was Julio Franko at 48 years

Oldest player to hit his 1st homerun was Bartolo Colon

Most homeruns after turning 40, with 79, is Barry Bonds

When Darryl Evans was 38 he smashed 40 dingers to become the oldest player to lead the league

Barry Bonds was intentionally walk 688 times

Oldest player to homer in a World Series game was 39 year old David Ross

September 8, 1916 Wally Schang became the first player to homer from both sides of the plate in a game. It wouldn't happen again until Augie Galan did it on June 25, 1937

Eddie Murray would homer from both sides of the plate in a game a record 11 times

MORE FAMOUS FIRST

1st expansion team player to start an All-Star game was Marlins outfielder Gary Sheffield in 1993

1st player to hit a pinch hit grand slam on his first MLB at bat was Jeremy Hermida on August 31, 2005

1st player to play 162 games without hitting into a double play was Astros Hall of Famer Craig Biggio

1st African American General Manager was Bob Watson (Astros)

1st batter to have more RBIs than games played was George Brett, 118 ribbies in 117 games in 1980

1st man to have 700 at-bats in a year was Willie Wilson, 1980

1st relief pitcher to save 40+ back to back was Dan Quisenberry

1st rookie to have 100 RBIs and score 100 runs was Carlos Beltran in 1999

1st team to sell hot dogs at a game was the New York Giants

1st team to sell nachos at a game was the Rangers

1st person on the cover of Sports Illustrated was Braves Eddie Matthews

1st person(s) on cover of Sport Magazine was Joe DiMaggio and Joe Jr

1st Cuban elected to the Hall of Fame was Negro League legend Martin Dihigo, considered the greatest all-around player EVER. He played everywhere except catcher

1st relief pitcher inducted into the Hall was Hoyte Wilhelm

1st relief pitcher to win the Cy Young and MVP awards the same year was Rollie Fingers

1st catcher to squat behind the plate was Buck Ewing

1st man to hit safely in all 7 games of a World Series was Braves Mark Lemke

1st player to win two Triple Crown Awards was Rogers Hornsby

1st A.L. player to win two was Ted Williams

1st pitcher to win back-to-back pitching Triple Crowns was Lefty Grove

1st pitcher to win the pitcher Triple Crown was Christy Mathewson

1st man to win two Cy Young Awards was Lefty Gomez

1st to win three was Sandy Koufax

1st to win four was Steve Carlton

1st to win five was Roger Clemens

1st to win six, Roger Clemens

1st to win four back-to-back-to-back-to-back was Greg Maddux

1st to win one in each league, Gaylord Perry

1st brothers to win, Gaylord and Jim Perry

1st man to win 2 MVP awards Rogers Hornsby

1st to win 3 MVPs Jimmy Foxx

1st to win 4, 5, 6, and 7 MVPs Barry Bonds

1st pitcher to win MVP Walter Johnson

1st player to receive 100% of the votes for the Hall of Fame, Mariano Rivera

1st World Series was played in 1903, Boston Americans beat the Pirates in the best 0f 9 games

1st batter in the 1st World Series was Ginger Beaumont

PICK A NUMBER IN MLB

1. 292 players have hit for the cycle (single, double, triple, and homerun in same game)

2. 116 players have homered in their first at bat in the majors

3. 224 players have hit inside the park homeruns (ball doesn.t go over the fence)

4. 47 players hit homeruns in their last major league at bat

5. 30 players hit a homer on the very first pitch they saw in the majors

6. 23 players have tossed perfect games (no hits, no walks, no errors)

7. 281 have thrown no hitters (no hits)

8. 75 have thrown 9 pitches for 9 strikes and 3 outs in an inning

9. 69 pitchers have thrown a gopher (homerun) ball to the first batter they faced in the majors

10. 13 perfect games were lost on the 27th batter (9 innings x 3 batters)

11. 6 batters were intentionally walked with bases loaded (THAT is respect)

12. May 7, 2017 there was 48 strike outs in an 18 inning game (Cubs/Yankees)

13. 15 triple plays, unassisted (1 fielder puts out 3 runners)

14. 4 times there has been 3 errors on the same play

15. 8 stolen bases by a team in the same inning

16. 52 times a player has stolen 2B, 3B, and home in the same inning

17. 11 times a player has stolen home twice in the same game

THE ABCs OF CAREER
HOME RUNS

A	HANK AARON	755
B	BOBBY BONDS	762
C	JOE CARTER	396
D	ANDRE DAWSON	436
E	DARRYL EVANS	414
F	JIMMY FOXX	534
G	KEN GRIFFEY JR	630
H	FRANK HOWARD	382
I	PETE INCAVIGLIA	183
J	REGGIE JACKSON	563
K	HARMON KILLEBREW	573
L	GREG LUZINSKI	307
M	WILLIE MAYS	660
N	GRAIG NETTLES	390
O	MEL OTT	511
P	TONY PEREZ	379
Q	JAMIE QUIRK	43
R	BABE RUTH	714
S	MIKE SCHMIDT	548
T	FRANK THOMAS	521

U	WILLIE UPSHAW	123
V	GREG VAUGHN	355
W	TED WILLIAMS	521
X	NONE	
Y	CARL YAZSTRZEMSKI	452
Z	TODD ZEILE	253

HOMERUN LEADERS BY THE STATE

ALABAMA	HANK AARON	755
ALASKA	RANDY KUTCHER	10
ARIZONA	HANK LEIBER	101
ARKANSAS	BROOKS ROBINSON	268
CALIFORNIA	TED WILLIAMS	521
COLORADO	JOHNNY FREDRICK	85
CONNETICUT	MO VAUGHN	328
D.C.	DON MONEY	176
DELAWARE	RANDY BUSH	96
FLORIDA	ANDRE DAWSON	436
GEORGIA	FRANK THOMAS	521
HAWAII	MIKE LUM	90
IDAHO	HARMON KILLEBREW	573
ILLINOIS	GREG LUZINSKI	307
INDIANA	GIL HODGES	370
IOWA	HAL TROSKY	228
KANSAS	BOB HORNER	218
KENTUCKY	JAY BUHNER	310
LOUISIANA	MEL OTT	511
MAINE	DEL BISSONETTE	66

MARYLAND	BABE RUTH	714
MASSACHUSETTS	RICHIE HEBNER	203
MICHIGAN	KIRK GIBSON	255
	JOHN MAYBERRY	255
MINNESOTA	DAVE WINFIELD	465
MISSISSIPPI	DAVE PARKER	339
MISSOURI	YOGI BERRA	358
MONTANA	JOHN LOWENSTEIN	116
NEBRASKA	WADE BOGGS	118
NEVADA	MARTY CORDOVA	122
NEW		
HAMPSHIRE	PHIL PLANTIER	91
NEW MEXICO	RALPH KINER	369
NEW JERSEY	GOOSE GOSLIN	248
NEW YORK	ALEX RODRIGUEZ	696
NORTH		
CAROLINA	JIM RAY HART	170
NORTH		
DAKOTA	KEN HUNT	33
OHIO	MIKE SCHMIDT	548
OKLAHOMA	MICKEY MANTLE	536
OREGAN	DAVE KINGMAN	442
PENNSYLVANIA	REGGIE JACKSON	563
RHODE ISLAND	GABBY HARNETT	236

SOUTH CAROLINA	JIM RICE	382
SOUTH DAKOTA	DAVE COLLINS	32
TENNESSEE	VADA PINSON	256
TEXAS	FRANK ROBINSON	586
UTAH	DUKE SIMS	100
VERMONT	CARLTON FISK	376
VIRGINIA	WILLIE HORTON	325
WASHINGTON	RON SANTO	342
WEST VIRGINIA	GEORGE BRETT	317
WISCONSIN	AL SIMMONS	307
WYOMING	MIKE DEVEREAUX	105

THE ABCs OF MOST WINS AS A PITCHER

A	GROVER CLEVELAND ALEXANDER	373
B	BERT BLYLEVEN	287
C	ROGER CLEMENS	345
D	HOOKS DAUSS	203
E	DENNIS ECKERSLEY	197
F	BOB FELLER	266
G	PUD GALVIN	365
H	CARL HUBBELL	253
I	HISASHI IWAKUMA	63
J	WALTER JOHNSON	417
K	JERRY KOOSMAN	222
L	TED LYONS	260
M	CHRISTY MATHEWSON	373
N	KID NICHOLS	362
O	AL ORTH	204
P	EDDIE PLANK	326
Q	JACK QUINN	247
R	NOLAN RYAN	324
S	WARREN SPAHN	363
T	FRANK TANANA	240

U	GEORGE UHLE	200
V	JUSTIN VERLANDER (active)	219
W	MICKEY WELCH	307
X	NONE	
Y	CY YOUNG	511
Z	TOM ZACHARY	186

MOST WINS BY STATE

ALABAMA	DON SUTTON	324
ALASKA	CURT SCHILLING	216
ARIZONA	JOHN DENNY	123
ARKANSAS	A.J. BURNETT	164
CALIFORNIA	TOM SEAVER	311
COLORADO	ROY HALLADAY	203
CONNECTICUT	CHARLES NAGY	129
DELAWARE	CHRIS SHORT	135
FLORIDA	STEVE CARLTON	329
GEORGIA	JIM BAGBY	127
HAWAII	CHARLIE HOUGH	216
IDAHO	LARRY JACKSON	194
ILLINOIS	ROBIN ROBERTS	286
INDIANA	TOMMY JOHN	288
IOWA	BOB FELLER	266
KANSAS	WALTER JOHNSON	417
KENTUCKY	GUS WEYHING	264
LOUISIANA	TED LYONS	260
MAINE	KID MADDEN	54
MARYLAND	LEFTY GROVE	300
MASSACHUSETTS	TIM KEEFE	342
MICHIGAN	FRANK TANANA	241
MINNESOTA	JACK MORRIS	254

MISSISSIPPI	GUY BUSH	176
MISSOURI	PUD GALVIN	365
MONTANA	DAVE McNALLY	184
NEBRASKA	PETE ALEXANDER	373
NEVADA	BARRY ZITO	165
NEW HAMPSHIRE	MIKE FLANAGAN	167
NEW JERSEY	HANK BOROWY	108
NEW MEXICO	WADE BLASINGAME	45
NEW YORK	WARREN SPAHN	363
NORTH CAROLINA	GAYLORD PERRY	314
NORTH DAKOTA	RICK HELLING	93
OHIO	CY YOUNG	511
OKLAHOMA	JESSE BARNES	152
OREGAN	CLIFF CHAMBERS	48
PENNSYLVANIA	CHRISTY MATHEWSON	373
RHODE ISLAND	CLEM LABINE	77
SOUTH CAROLINA	BOBBY BOLIN	88
SOUTH DAKOTA	FLOYD BANNISTER	134
TENNESSEE	TOM BOLTON and	
	JOHNNY BEAZLER	31
TEXAS	GREG MADDUX	355
UTAH	BRUCE HURST	145
VERMONT	RAY FISHER	100
VIRGINIA	EPPA RIXEY	266
WASHINGTON	ED BRANDT	121
WEST VIRGINIA	WILBUR COOPER	216
WISCONSIN	KID NICHOLS	362
WYOMING	TOM BROWNING	123
D.C.	JOHNNY KLIPPSTEIN	101

MORE USELESS INFORMATION YOU MAY NOT HAVE KNOWN

On June 5, 1994, Tony Phillips, of the Tigers, led off for his team with a homerun. The Twins leadoff batter, Chuck Knoblauch also hit a leadoff homerun.

On September 8, 1995, Chuck Knoblauch led off for the Twins with a leadoff homer and the Tiger's leadoff batter also hit a homerun, his name was Tony Phillips.

Luis Aparacio hit his first homerun off of Tom Lasorda

Hank Aaron hit 17 homeruns off of Don Drysdale

Ernie Banks slammed 15 homers off Robin Roberts

Johnny Bench victimized Steve Carlton AND Don Sutton for 12 dingers

Albert "Chief" Bender was a full-blooded Chippewa, born on a reservation in Minnesota

1942 the Indians named 24 year old Lou Boudreau as their new manager, who was 24 years old. He was also married to the owners daughter.

Roger Bresnahan, in 1907, introduced shin guards to the game

Lou Brock, a rookie for the Cubs, got his first hit in the majors off of Robin Roberts. He got his 3000th hit against the Cubs, who had traded him in 1963.

When Mordecai Brown was a boy he lost all but one inch of his right index finger, thus the nickname "Three Fingered Brown". He perfected the curve ball with his right hand and threw his way into the Hall-of-Fame

Roy Campanella was the N.L. MVP in 1951, 1953, and 1955, but in 1958 he was paralyzed in a car accident, taking away one of, if not the, best catchers in MLB.

Rod Carew bathed his bats in alcohol

Hall-of-Fame Umpire Carl Hubbard started his umpiring career after a Hall-of- Fame NFL career. He was the person that suggested the four man umpiring crew

In 1963 N.L. MVP Sandy Koufax and A.L. MVP and NFL MVP Jim Brown all three wore number 32

August 4, 1983 while warming up in pre-game Dave Winfield threw a ball that hit a seagull and killed it. The local police arrested him after the game and charged him with animal cruelty, but charges were later dropped. Yankee manager Billy Martin told the press, "They wouldn't say he hit that bird on purpose if they saw some of his throws he's made this year."

Until 1930 a batted ball that bounced over the fence was ruled a homerun, so the A.L. changed the rule and started calling it a ground rule double. In 1931 the N.L. followed suit. Interesting note, NONE of Babe Ruth's homeruns were bounced over.

Stan Musial finished his career with 3,630 hits. 1,815 were hit at home and 1,815 were hit on the road.

In 2009 CC Sabathia, a Yankee, and Cliff Lee, a Phillie, faced each other twice. Both were their respective leagues Cy Young Award Winners and both were traded to the Indians before the 2010 season.

Also in 2009, on Opening Day, D'Back's Tony Clark and Rockie's Felipe Lopez both hit 2 homeruns, both hit 1 right handed and 1 left handed. In the same game

Babe Ruth batted .344 in his career, but, as a pinch hitter he hit .167

Asked when he thought he'd ever get a homerun, Gaylord Perry answered, "They'll put a man on the moon before I ever hit a homerun!" That was in 1963, on July 20, 1969 Neil Armstrong walked on the moon, 20 minutes later Gaylord Perry hit the only homerun of his career.

The 70 dingers Mark McGwire smashed in 1998 traveled 29,958 feet, that's higher than Mount Everest

All MLB baseballs are rubbed in a special "mud" that takes off the slick shine. One company and one only does this. It is a special mud collected from where the company's owner lives. No one else knows where it comes from.

In 1920, Edd Roush was ejected from a game for falling asleep, IN THE OUTFIELD

July 17, 1914 the Giants was playing the Pirates in a tight game. In the 22nd inning Giants outfielder Red Murray went to catch a fly ball and was knocked out by a bolt of lightning

In 1920 there was no such thing as "political correctness", so when Dummy Hoy batted against Dummy Taylor it marked the 1st time that two deaf players faced each other in a MLB game

In the three years Sammy Sosa hit 60 or more homers, he never won a homerun title

Glen Gorbus, on August 1, 1957, threw a baseball 445 feet and ten inches! Not only a world record, it would go out of every park in the majors

The Phillies once won a game by forfeit in New York because the Giant fans were throwing snowballs at them

FAMOUS DATES IN THE GRAND OLD GAME

1. APRIL 15, 1947 Jackie Robinson breaks the color barrier to become the first African American to play MLB since the 1880's

2. APRIL 8, 1974 Hank Aaron breaks Babe Ruth's career homerun record with # 715

3. APRIL 29, 1986 Roger Clemens strikes out 20 Mariners in one game

4. MAY 4, 2018 Albert Pujols hits his 3000th career base hit

5. MAY 5, 1978 Pete Rose collects his 3000th career hit

6. MAY 6, 1982 Gaylord Perry wins his 300th career game

7. MAY 13, 1958 Stan Musial gets career hit #3000

8. MAY 17, 1970 Hank Aaron collects hit #3000

9. JUNE 4, 2009 Randy Johnson gets career win #300

10. JUNE 13, 2003 Roger Clemens picks up career win # 300

11. JUNE 19, 1942 Paul Waner hits his 3000th career hit

12. JUME 19, 2015 Alex Rodriguez enters the 3000 hit club

13. JUNE 28, 2007 Craig Biggio hits # 3000 of his career

14. JUNE 30, 1995 switch hitting power slugger Eddie Murray gets hit # 3000

15. JULY 9, 2011 Derek Jeter joins the 3000 hit club

16. JULY 13, 1963 Early Wynn gets win # 300

17. JULY 15, 2005 Rafael Palmeiro becomes a member of the 3000 hit club

18. JULY 18, 1970 The "Say Hey Kid', Willie Mays gets his 3000th career hit

19. JULY 25, 1941 Lefty Grove collects career # 300 win

20. JULY 30, 2017 Adrian Beltre hits his 3000th career hit

21. JULY 31, 1990 Nolan Ryan picks up his 300th career win

22. AUGUST 4, 1985 Rod Carew hits # 3000

23. AUGUST 5, 2007 Tom Glavine wins # 300

24. AUGUST 6, 1999 Padre Tony Gwynn collects his 3000th career hit

25. AUGUST 7, 1999 Wade Boggs hits his 3000th hit

26. AUGUST 7, 2004, Greg Maddux wins his 300th game

27. AUGUST 7, 2016 Ichiro Suzuki joins the 3000 hit club

28. AUGUST 11, 1961 Lefty Warren Spahn wins his 300th game

29. AUGUST 13, 1979 speedy Lou Brock connects for his 3000th hit

30. SEPTEMBER 9, 1992 Robin Yount gets # 3000 of his career

31. SEPTEMBER 9, 1979 Carl Yazstrzemski joins the elite 3000 hit club

32. SEPTEMBER 16, 1993 Dave Winfield joins the 3000 hit club

33. SEPTEMBER 16, 1996 Paul Molitor becomes a career 3000 hit man

34. SEPTEMBER 23, 1983 Steve Carlton wins # 300 of his career

35. SEPTEMBER 30, 1972 the great Roberto Clemente gets hit # 3000

36. SEPTEMBER 30, 1992 George Brett collects career hit 3000

37. OCTOBER 6, 1982 Gaylord Perry joins the 300 hit club

38. OCTOBER 7, 2001 Rickey Henderson gets his career hit # 3000

CAN YOU BELIEVE?

A. That a baseball that is hit by a bat accelerates at 3000 times the force of gravity? That is 30 times faster than a ballistic missile

B. The ball hit by Bobby Thompson in the 1951 game called "The shot heard around the world" has never been found?

C. On September 13, 2016 there were 1,122 dogs attending the Chicago White Sox Game?

D. In 1916, the Cubs and Reds played an entire 9 inning game with just one baseball?

E. Cal Ripken JR played 2,632 consecutive games from April 30, 1982 to September 9, 1998 without missing a single game?

F. Barry Bonds won 7 MVP awards? That's four more than the closest runner-up, of which there are 7 that won 3 each

G. Moises Alou and Jorge Posada would pee on their hands for a "perfect" grip on the bat? Not sure how many high fives they received

H. A new baseball in a major league game averages lasting 6 to 7 pitches?

I.   A 17 year old girl once struck out Babe Ruth and Lou Gehrig on six pitches? Never say a girl can't play baseball

J.   The Seattle Mariners are owned by the Nintendo Company?

K.   On July 27, 1930 Ken Ash was brought in for relief for the Reds in the 8th inning. There were two runners on base. On the first pitch, the batter hit into a triple play. The Reds then rallied at their at bat in the 9th and won the game 6-5. Ash got the win, with one pitch? What a workhorse

L.   A player once bit himself on the butt in a game? In 1923 Clarence Blethen was a rookie pitcher for the Red Sox. When he was pitching he would put his false teeth in his hip pocket. In one game he was running the bases and forgot about his chompers when he slid into the base. He remembered where they were when he slid, because they clamped down on his back side.

M.   Bill Voiselle always wore number 96 on his jersey, because he was from 96, South Carolina and he wanted to wear his hometown's name?

N.   Jack McCarthy set a record in 1905 while playing for the Cubs that still stands alone. He threw out 3 baserunners at home plate in the same inning?

O.   The 1968 All-Star Game was the first played indoors, at the Astrodome, and it is the ONLY one without an RBI, even though the N.L. won 1-0? How? The N.L. put a lead off runner on, the next batter singled the runner to third, then the next batter hit into a double-play, scoring the runner from third, BUT an RBI cannot be awarded on a fielder's choice.

The game ended 1-0. The lone run was named MVP. His name was Willie Mays.

P. Warren Spahn retired with 363 wins and 363 hits?

Q. On July 17, 1990 the Twins pulled 2 triple plays against the Red Sox, and still lost the game?

R. On July 18, 1990 the Twins and Red Sox combined to hit into a record number of double plays? The Twins lost that game too

S. Joe Maddon was the manager that finally broke the curse of the Cubs by winning the World Series in 2016?

T. Terry Francona managed the Red Sox to the title in 2004 breaking the Curse of the Bambino placed on them 86 years earlier?

U. The Indians have not won a series since 1948? Their manager is Terry Francona

V. Gene Mauch won 1900 games as a manager from 1960 to 1987 and won the Manager of the Year 3 times, without ever winning a pennant?

W. Billy Martin won 55% of the games he managed, 2 A.L. pennants, and 1 World Series?

X. Leo "The Lip" Durocher won over 2000 games, 3 pennants, and the 1954 Series?

Y.   Danny Murtaugh played for the Pirates for 9 years and then managed them to the 1960 and 1971 Series titles?

Z.   Miller Huggins won 3 titles with the Yankees, but passed away at the age of 51 after winning the 1928 title? When Babe Ruth once told him he was going to "bite his head off", Huggins replied, "Go ahead, then you'll have more brains in your stomach than you do in your head."

AA. Bill McKechnie was the first manager to win a series with 2 different teams He won 3 pennants and 2 series.

BB. The second manager to win 3 pennants with 3 different teams was Dick Williams? He took the Red Sox over in 1967, a year after being dead last in the A.L. and won the '67 pennant. He won back-to-back series with the Athletics in 1972-1973. He would later take the Padres to their first pennant.

CC. Bruce Bochy managed the Giants to series titles in 2010, 2012, and 2014?

DD. Bucky Harris was the youngest manager to win a series title? He led the Senators to the 1924 series and would not return to the series until 1947 when he won his second title as the Yankee's manager. He won 2159 games.

EE. Tommy Lasorda won over 1600 games, 4 pennants, and 2 world series (1981 and 1988)?

FF. Bobby Cox led the Braves to 5 pennants and 1 series championship. He also took the Blue Jays to a Division title in 1985?

GG. Earl Weaver won 4 pennants and 1 series with the Orioles?

HH. Walt Alston won over 2000 games and 4 series titles (1 in Brooklyn and 3 in Los Angeles)?

II. Sparky Anderson won over 2194 games and 3 series (2 with the Reds, 1 with the Tigers)?

JJ. Joe Torre won 2326 games, 6 pennants and 4 series?

KK. Tony LaRussa won 2728 games, 6 pennants and 3 series?

LL. John McGraw won 2763 games, 10 pennants, and 3 series?

MM. In 53 years as manager for the Athletics, Connie Mack won 3,731 games, 9 pennants, and 5 series?

NN. Joe McCarthy won 9 pennants and 7 series?

OO. Casey Stengal won 10 pennants and 7 series?

BASEBALL'S SMARTEST HITTERS

1. Tony Gwynn; collected 3,141 hits in 20 seasons, won 8 batting titles, never hit below .300, and had nearly twice as many walks as strikeouts

2. Rogers Hornsby: didn't reach 3,000 hits, but never batted below .300, and hit .400 three different times

3. Stan Musial:22 years, 3,630 hits, 1,599 walks, and 696 strikeouts. Stan the Man walked 2 ½ times more than he struck out

4. Hank Aaron: 25 All-Star games, 3,771 hits, 755 homeruns, and had 19 more walks than he did strike outs

5. Babe Ruth: a career .342 batter, 714 homeruns, 1,300 strike outs, 2,062 walks, and 7 World Series titles

6. Barry Bonds: a .298 hitter, .444 on-base %, 2,935 hits, 762 homers, and 2,558 walks. Steroids may make muscles and help one hit a ball farther, BUT it doesn't make the bat speed faster nor increase the eyesight. Put him in the Hall

7. Pete Rose: Okay, he bet on baseball, who cares? He bet on his team? Did they throw any games? Here's the FACTS,

4,256 hits and a walk-to-strikeout ratio of 2-1! Besides, who else runs to first on a walk?

8. Ted Williams: A .344 hitter, 521 homeruns, last man to bat over .400 in a season, only one season under .300 (forced his team to give him a cut in pay the next year), 2,021 walks, and 709 strikeouts. They delivered his shipment of bats one year, he picked a few out and told them they weren't the correct. They went and weighed them and they were .0019 off. Who the hell would have noticed that?

9. Albert Pujols: Regularly hits .300 or better, over 500 dingers and counting, more walks than strikeouts, 3 MVP awards, and 1 batting title. Considered to be the pickiest and most patient batter in the MLB

WHERE ARE THEY SUPPOSED TO PLAY

1. Trevor Hoffman was drafted to play shortstop

2. Eddie Murray and Dave Parker were drafted as catchers

3. Mike Piazza and Tim Wakefield were originally first basemen

4. Buddy Bell came in as a second baseman

5. Jim Thome, Mike Schmidt, Wade Boggs, and Chipper Jones were drafted as shortstops

6. Manny Ramerez and Jose Canseco were supposed to have been third basemen

7. Dave Stieb was considered an outfield prospect

8. Dave Winfield, Mark McGuire, Dave Kingman, and Ryan Klesko were to be pitchers

MORE WORDS OF WISDOM

"On my tombstone I want written, 'The sorest loser that ever played'," Earl Weaver

"A baseball player is a necessary evil," Sparky Anderson

"How old would you be if you didn't know how old you were?", Satchel Paige

"Age is a question of mind over matter. If you don't mind, it doesn't matter." Satchel Paige

"Sometimes I sits and thinks, and sometimes I just sits." Satchell Paige

"I never had a job. I always played baseball." Satchell Paige

"He slides into second base with a stand up double!", play-by-play announcer Jerry Coleman

"It's a hard hit to the outfield. The fielder is going back, back and catches the ball and hits the wall head first, and it's rolling back to the infield.", yep, Jerry Coleman

"Why does everyone stand up and sing 'Take Me out to the Ballgame' when their already here?" Larry Anderson

"When I'm on the field I pray two things, please God, don't let them hit it to me and please don't hit it to Sax (Steve Sax)," Pedro Guerro

"It's hard to beat a person who never gives up," Babe Ruth

"Baseball is dull to people with dull minds," Red Barber

"A baseball game is simply a nervous breakdown divided into innings," Earl Wilson

"Mister, that boy couldn't hit the ground if he fell out of a plane," Casey Stengal

"We are a much improved team this year, now we lose in extra innings," Casey Stengal about the Mets

"What does it take to make a successful manager? A sense of humor and a good bull pen," Whitey Herzog

"To be contenders we need two players, Babe Ruth and Sandy Koufax," Whitey Herzog

"There is no secret to managing. You put the best players in the game and watch them play," Sparky Anderson

"My job is to give my team a chance to win," Nolan Ryan

"When baseball is no longer fun, it's no longer a game." Joe Dimaggio

MORE NICKNAMES

Devon "Devo" White

Kent "Bones" Tekulve

Doug "Eye Chart" Gnosds

Charles "Chick" Hafey

"Skuz" Ross Grimsley

Daniel "Rusty" Staub

Hoyte "Old Tilt" Wilhelm

Ray "Cracker" Schalk

Billy "Jaguar" Myers

Steve "Mr Perfect" Garvey

Dave "Beauty" Bancroft

"Mad Russian" Lou Novikoff

Tony "EL Gato" Pena

John "Pepper" Martin

"King" Carl Hubbell

Dick "Turk" Farrell

George "Boomer" Scott

Frank "Tater" Lary

"Jungle" Jim Rivera

Randy "Big Unit" Johnson

Leon "Daddy Wags" Wagner

Doug "Rooster" Rader

William "Gates" Brown

"Wahoo" Sam Crawford

Jim "Emu" Kern

Harry "The Hat" Walker

"AO" Amos Otis

Jim "Gumby" Gantner

Chris "Spuds" Sabo

Frank "Husk" Chance

"Joker" Joe Randa

Craig "Pig Pen" Biggio

"Smilin" Stan Hack

"Toy Cannon" Jim Wynn

Harry "Stinky" Davis

Vida Blue "Heat"

"Fordham Flash" Frankie Frisch

Steve "Psycho" Lyons

Joe "Ducky" Medwick

Mart "Slats" Marion

Dave "Hendu" Henderson

Calvin "Pokey" Reese

Pete "Charlie Hustle" Rose

Orel "Bulldog" Hershiser

Eddie "The Brat" Stankey

"Wild Horse of the Osage" Pepper Martin

Jerry "The Governor" Brown

Honus "The Flying Dutchman" Wagner

Cecil "Big Daddy" Fielder

Walter "Rabbit" Maranville

Dick "Shortwave" Bartell

Jim "Mudcat" Grant

Mickey "The Commerce Comet" Mantle

Tony "Push 'Em Up" Lazziri

Ryan "Rhino" Sandberg

"Dr Strange Glove" Dick Stuart

Jeff "Bags" Bagwell

BEST THINGS TO EAT
AT THE BALLPARKS

Oakland Coliseum, section 104, "Ribs and Things"

Tropicana Field, any concession in the stadium, the "Cuban Sandwich"

Kauffman Stadium, anywhere in the stadium, "Belfonte Ice Cream"

Comerica Park, section 122, "Chicken Shawarma Nachos"

White Sox Field, sections 104, 127, 142, and 529, "Elote/Corn on, or off, the Cobb"

Blue Jays Centre, section 141, "Churro Poutine"

Cardinals Stadium, section 144, "The Food Network Hot Dog Bar"

Angels Stadium, section 223, "Chronic Tacos"

Dodger Stadium, anywhere in the park, "Super Dodger Dog"

Reds Ball Park, anywhere in the park, "Skyline Chili"

Coors Field, at the Rooftop, "Chuburger"

Fenway Park, any concession, "Fenway Frank"

Rangers Park, section 141 "Most Valuable Taco" or at all concessions "The Boom Stick"

(A two foot long hot dog)

Brewers Park you can get "Bratchos"

Diamondbacks Field, sections 114 and 123 has "Churro Dogs 2.0"

Nationals Park, sections 109, 140, and 317, "Ben's Chili Bowl"

Phillies Park, section 104, "Cheesesteak"

Astro's Park, section 125 and 406, "Texas Smoke"

STATES AND HOW MANY PLAYERS THEY SENT TO MLB

CALIFORNIA 2,304
PENSYLVANIA 1, 431
NEW YORK 1,207
ILLINOIS...1,062
OHIO 1,039
TEXAS..938
MASSACHUSETTS 664
MISSOURI...612
FLORIDA 563
NEW JERSEY 437
MICHIGAN 434
NORTH CAROLINA 416
INDIANA...380
GEORGIA..378
ALABAMA 336
TENNESSEE..318
MARYLAND 313
VIRGINIA.. 296
KENTUCKY..288
OKLAHOMA...266
LOUISIANA 261
WISCONSIN..244
IOWA 222

TOP 10 FOREIGN COUNTRIES

DOMINICAN REPUBLIC 757
VENEZUALA 405
PUERTO RICO 267
CANADA...255
CUBA...212
MEXICO 129
UNITED KINGDOM...49
IRELAND...47
GERMANY 42
AUSTRALIA 31

MORE DATES TO REMEMBER

1.   JUNE 13, 1948.....Babe Ruth made his final appearance at Yankee Stadium

2.   July 4, 1939.....Lou Gehrig gave his famous "I'm the luckiest man alive" speech

3.   July 6 1933.....The first All-Star Game is played in Chicago's Comisky Park. 20 players, both managers, and 3 of the 4 coaches are all future Hall-of-Famers

4.   JULY 10, 1934.....Carl Hubbell struck out Babe Ruth, Lou Gehrig, Jimmie Foxx, Al Simmons, and Joe Cronin in succession, Bill Dickey singled and Lefty Gomez then went down swinging. All seven batters are in the Cooperstown

5.   AUGUST 18, 1951...Eddie Gaedel made his 1st and only at bat and walked. He stood 3'7"

6.   SEPTEMBER 11, 1985.....Pete Rose passes Ty Cobb on the all-time hit list

7.   OCTOBER 1, 1961.....Roger Maris breaks the single season homerun mark by hitting number 61

8.   OCTOBER 3, 1947…..Cookie Lavagetto breaks up Bill Beven's no-hitter in the 9th inning as the last batter

9.   OCTOBER 8, 1956…..Don Larsen throws the first no-hitter and perfect game in World Series history

10.   OCTOBER 10, 1920…..Bill Wambaganes pulls the only unassisted triple play in World Series history

11.   OCTOBER 18, 1977……Reggie Jackson hit 3 homeruns on 3 pitches

AND THEY SAID

In a game against the Cubs there was a threat made that if Jackie Robinson played he would be shot. Pee Wee Reece spoke up and suggested, "Why don't we all wear number 42 and then they won't know which one of us to shoot."

When asked by a reporter why he was not satisfied with his .401 average he replied, "If you failed to do what you were paid to do, six and a half out of every ten jobs you were assigned, would you be happy?"

When Casey Stengal chose a catcher as his first draft pick for the Mets he was asked why. His answer, "If you don't have a catcher, you have a lot of dropped ball, there's nobody behind the plate."

Danny Ozark, while coaching the Phillies, once told the press that, "Half of the game is 90% mental."

Earl Weaver said, "The secret of a good manager is to have 13 men like you more than 12 who don't like you at all. You must keep a majority, however slight, in your favor."

Yogi Berra, when asked if he thought he could be a manager, replied, "You can observe a lot about the game just by watching."

After Jackie Robinson established himself as a player, one opposing player said he would slide into his mother to break up a double play. When asked this, Jackie answered, "Yes."

HOMERUN MILESTONES FOR THE TOP TWO HITTERS

BARRY BONDS

Homerun number 1, June 4, 1986, off of Brave Craig McMurt

"   "   100, July 12, 1990, off Padre Andy Benes

"   "   200, July 8, 1993, off Phillie Jose Del Leon

"   "   300, April 27, 1996, off Marlin John Burkett

"   "   400, August 23, 1998 off Marlin Kirt Ojala

"   "   500, April 17, 2001 off Dodger Terry Adams

"   "   600, August 9, 2002 off Pirate Kip Wells

"   "   700, May 20, 2004 off Athletic Brad Halsey

"   "   715, May 28, 2006 off Rockie Byung-Hyun Kim

"   "   756, August 7, 2007 off Nationals Mike Bacsik

"   "   762, September 5, 2007 off Rockie Ubaldo Jimenez

HANK AARON

Homerun number 1 April 23, 1954 off Cardinal Vic Raschi

    "   "   100 August 15, 1957 off Don Gross

    "   "   200 July 3, 1960 off Cardinal Ron Cline

    "   "   300 April 19, 1963, off Mets Roger Craig

    "   "   400 April 20, 1966 off Phillie Bo Belinsky

    "   "   500 July 14, 1968 off Giant Mike McCormick

    "   "   600 April 27, 1971 off Giant Gaylord Perry

    "   "   700 July 21, 1973 off Phillie Ken Brett

    "   "   714 April 4, 1974 off Red Jack Billingham

    "   "   715 April 8, 1974 off Dodger Al Downing

    "   "   755 July 20, 1976 off Angel Dick Drago

THE TALL AND SHORT
OF BASEBALL

	Tallest Players	Shortest Players
1.	Jon Rauch 6' 11"	Eddie Gaedel 3' 7"
2.	Randy Johnson 6' 10"	Stubby Magner 5' 3"
3.	Eric Hillman 6' 10"	Bob Emmerich 5' 3"
4.	Chris Young 6' 10"	Jess Cortazzo 5' 3"
5.	Mark Hendrickson 6' 9"	Yo-Yo Davallo 5' 3"
6.	Richie Sexson 6' 8"	Mich McCormick 5' 3"
7.	Tyler Glasnow 6' 8"	Wee Willie Keeler 5' 4"
8.	Dellin Betances 6' 8"	Rabbit Maranville 5' 5"
9.	Doug Fister 6' 8"	Freddie Patek 5' 5"
10.	Aaron Judge 6'7"	Hack Wilson 5'6"
11.	Frank Howard 6'7"	Phil Rizzuto 5'6"
12.	Nate Frieman 6'7"	Miller Huggins 5'6"
13.	Dave Winfield 6'6"	Joe Sewell 5'6"
14.	CC Sabathia 6'6"	Billy Hamilton 5'6"
15.	Giancarlo Stanton 6'6"	Jose Altve 5'6"
16.	Dave Kingman 6'6"	
17.	Corey Hart 6'6"	
18.	Jameson Taillon 6'6"	
19.	Adam Dunn 6'6"	
20.	Darryl Strawberry 6'6"	
21.	Chuck Conners 6'6"	

SOME OF THE WORSE
PLAYERS EVER

1. Mario Mendoza 1974 – 1982 The man that set the "Mendoza Line" for batters

2. Bob Ueker 1962 – 1967 as a player he made a great announcer

3. Fred Merkle 1907 – 1926 Made one of the greatest "Bonehead" plays of all time

4. Marve Throneberry 1955-1963 a glove of steel

5. Tommy Lasorda 1954-1956 as a pitcher he was a hell of a manager

6. Michael Jordan 1994 the greatest basketball player ever, as a baseball player he was the greatest basketball player ever

7. Danny Ainge 1979-1981 as a shortstop he made a pretty good guard

"Every hitter likes fastballs just like everybody likes ice cream. But you don't like it when someone is stuffing it into you by the gallon.

That's how you feel when you face Nolan Ryan's throwing balls by you," Reggie Jackson

A young hitter was facing Walter Johnson and headed to the dugout, the umpire told him, "You only have two strikes, you still have one more." The batter replied, "You call it, I never saw the first two."

Satchel Paige once commented on Cool Papa Bell, "He hit a line drive right past my ear one day. I turned around and saw the ball hit him in the ass as he was sliding into second base."

Buck O'Neil I always gave the same answer when asked how fast was Cool Papa? "Faster that that!" he would answer

MOST WINS BY BROTHERS IN MLB

1. Phil and Joe Niekro with 539 wins

2. Gaylord and Jim Perry with 529 wins

3. Greg and Mike Maddux with 394 wins

4. Pedro and Ramon Martinez with 352 wins

5. Stan and Harry Covelski with 296 wins

6. Bob and Ken Forsch with 282 wins

7. Livan and Orlando Hernandez with 264 wins

8. Rick and Paul Reuschel with 230 wins

9. Al and Mark Leiter with 227 wins

10. Jesse and Virgil Barnes with 213 wins

11. Dizzy and Daffy Dean with 200 wins

12. Jeff and Jered Weaver with 200 wins

13.   Andy and Alan Benes with 184 wins

14.   Lindy and Von McDaniel with 148 wins

15.   Alex and Walt Kellner with 101 wins

16.   Rick and Mickey Mahler with 100 wins

MY ALL – DECADE TEAMS

	NL(National League)		AL (American League)	NNL (National Negro League)	
	1910 – 1919			1920 - 1929	
C	Louis Santop	NNL	Biz Mackey	NNL	
1B	Frank Chance	NL	Lou Gehrig	AL	
2B	Nap Lajoie	NL	Rogers Hornsby	NL	
3B	John McGraw	NL	Pie Traynor	NL	
SS	Honus Wagner	AL	John Henry Lloyd	NNL	
LF	Turkey Srearns	NNL	Mule Settles	NNL	
CF	Oscar Charleston	NNL	Oscar Charleston	NNL	
RF	Sam Crawford	AL	Babe Ruth	AL	
RHP	Rube Foster	NNL	Walter Johnson	AL	
LHP	Babe Ruth	AL	Lefty Grove	AL	
RP	Cy Young	AL	Grover Alexander	NL	

	1930 – 1939			1940 – 1949	
C	Josh Gibson	NNL	Yogi Berra	AL	
1B	Lou Gehrig	AL	Buck Leonard	NNL	
2B	Charles Gehringer	AL	Jackie Robinson	NL	
3B	Pie Traynor	NL	Ray Dandridge	NNL	
SS	Joe Cronin	NL	Pee Wee Reece	NL	
LF	Joe Medwick	NL	Ted Williams	AL	

CF	Cool Papa Bell	NNL	Joe DiMaggio	AL
RF	Martin Dihigo	NNL	Stan Musial	NL
RHP	Satchel Paige	NNL	Bob Feller	AL
LHP	Carl Hubbell	NL	Hal Newhouser	AL
RP	Syl Johnson	AL	Hugh Casey	NL

	1950 – 1959		**1960 – 1969**	
C	Roy Campanella	NL	Joe Torre	NL
1B	Gil Hodges	NL	Harmon Killebrew	AL
2B	Nellie Fox	AL	Bill Mazeroski	NL
3B	Eddie Mathews	NL	Ken Boyer	NL
SS	Ernie Banks	NL	Luis Aparacio	AL
LF	Ted Williams	AL	Carl Yaztrzemski	AL
CF	Mickey Mantle	AL	Willie Mayes	NL
RF	Hank Aaron	NL	Roger Maris	NL
RHP	Bob Lemon	AL	Bob Gibson	NL
LHP	Warren Spahn	NL	Sandy Koufax	NL
RP	Hoyt Wilhelm	AL	Stu Miller	AL

	1970 – 1979		**1980 – 1989**	
C	Johnny Bench	NL	Gary Carter	NL
1B	Willie Stargill	NL	Eddie Murray	AL
2B	Rod Carew	AL	Lou Whitaker	AL
3B	Brooks Robinson	AL	Mike Schmidt	NL
SS	Dave Concepcion	NL	Ozzie Smith	NL
LF	Lou Brock	NL	Rickey Henderson	AL
CF	Cesar Cedeno	NL	Dale Murphy	NL
RF	Pete Rose	NL	Tony Gwynn	NL
RHP	Jim Palmer	AL	Dwight Gooden	NL

LHP	Steve Carlton	NL	Fernando Valenzuela	NL
RP	Rollie Fingers	AL	Lee Smith	NL
DH	N/A		Don Baylor	AL

1990 – 1999			2000 – 2009	
C	Juan Rodriguez	AL	Mike Piazza	NL
1B	Jeff Bagwell	NL	Albert Pujols	NL
2B	Ryne Sandberg	NL	Alfonso Soriano	AL
3B	Wade Boggs	AL	Chipper Jones	NL
SS	Alex Rodriguez	AL	Derek Jeter	AL
LF	Barry Bonds	NL	Barry Bonds	NL
CF	Ken Griffey Jr	AL	Torii Hunter	AL
RF	Larry Walker	NL	Vladimir Guerrero	AL
RHP	Greg Maddux	NL	Pedro Martinez	AL
LHP	Randy Johnson	Al	Randy Johnson	AL
RP	Trevor Hoffman	NL	Mariano Rivera	AL

TALLEST STARS

Randy Johnson	6'10"
Chris Young	6'10"
Frank Howard	6'7"
Dave Winfield	6'6"
Dave Kingman	6'6"
Chuck Connors	6'6"
Adam Dunn	6'6"
Darryl Strawberry"	6'6

SHORTEST STARS

Eddie Gaede	3'7"
Billy Hamilton	5'6"
Willie Keeler	5'4"
Rabbit Marienville	5'5"
Freddie Pate	5'5"
Hack Wilson	5'6"
Phil Rizzuto	5'6"
Joe Sewell	5'6"

ALL TIME LEADERS IN GROUNDING INTO DOUBLE PLAYS

1.	ALBERT	PUJOLS	386
2.	CAL	RIPKIN	350
3.	IVAN	RODRIGUEZ	337
4.	HANK	AARON	328
5.	CARL	YAZSTRZIMSKI	323
6.	DAVE	WINFIELD	319
7.	EDDIE	MURRAY	315
8.	JIM	RICE	315
9.	JULIO	FRANCO	312
10.	MIGUEL	CABRERA	309

GROUNDED INTO DPs IN
SEASON LEADERS

1.　　Jim Rice 36 in 1984

2.　　Jim Rice 35 in 1985

3.　　Billy Butler 32 in 2010

4.　　Ben Grieve 32 in 2000

5.　　Jackie Jensen 32 in 1954

6.　　Cal Ripkin Jr 32 in 1985

7.　　Miguel Tejada 32 in 2008

	ALL- JEWISH TEAM	ALL-PANAMANIAN TEAM
C	Mike Liebert Hal	Manny Sanguillan
1B	Hank Greenburgh	Rod Carew
2B	Ian Kinsler	Rennie Stennett
3B	Al Rosen	Hector Lopez
SS	Lou Boudreau	Ruben Tejada
LF	Ryan Braun	Carlos Lee
CF	Shawn Green	Roberto Kelly
RF	Kevin Youkillis	Ben Oglivie
LHP	Sandy Koufax	Bruce Chen
RHP	Steve Stone	Juan Berenger
RP	Joel Horlen	Mariano Rivera

	ALL IRISH TEAM	ALL CANADIAN TEAM
C	Tim McCarver	Russell Martin
1B	Steve Garvey	Joey Votto
2B	Joe McEwing	Jeff Heath
3B	Mark McGuire	Vladimir Guerro Jr
SS	Gene Michael	Terry Puhl
LF	Adam Dunn	Jason Bay
CF	Eric Byrnes	Larry Walker
RF	Paul O'Neil	George Selkirk
RHP	Nolan Ryan	Ferguson Jenkins
LHP	Dave McNally	James Paxton
RP	Tug McGraw	Eric Gagne
DH	Mike Sweeney	Justin Morneau

	ALL DOMINICAN TEAM	ALL MEXICAN
C	Tony Pena	Alex Trevino
1B	Albert Pujols	Adrian Gonzalez
2B	Robinson Cano	Bobby Avila
3B	Adrian Beltre	Vinny Castillo
SS	Hanley Ramirez	Juan Castro
LF	Manny Ramirez	Jorge Orta
CF	Sammy Sosa	Mel Alamada
RF	Vladimir Guerro Sr	Karim Garcia
RHP	Pedro Martinez	Ismael Valdez
RHP	Juan Maricha	Fernando Valenzuela
RP	Bartolo Colon	Joakim Soria
DH	David Ortiz	Aurilio Rodriguez

	ALL NATIVE AMERICAN TEAM	ALL JAPANESE TEAM
C	John Meyers	Kenji Johjima
1B	Rudy York	Akinori Iwamura
2B	Gene Locklear	Kazuo Matsui
3B	Pepper Martin	Norihiro Nakamura
SS	Bob Neighbors	Munenori Kawasaki
LF	Pepper Martin	Ichiro Suzuki
CF	Jacoby Ellsbury	Tsuyoshi Shinjo
RF	Bob Johnson	Norichika Aoki
DH	Roy Johnson	Hideki Matsui
SP	Allie Reynolds	Masanori Nurakami
SP	Charles Bender	Masato Yoshi
RP	Cal McLish	Hideo Nomo

	ALL CUBAN	ALL PUERTO RICAN
C	Yasmani Grandal	Ivan Rodriguez
1B	Rafael Palmeiro	Orlando Cepeda
2B	Lourdes Gurriel Jr	Roberto Alomar
3B	Tony Perez	Mike Lowell
SS	Bert Campaneris	Sandy Alomar Sr
LF	Yandy Diaz	Bernie Williams
CF	Yasiel Puig	Carlos Beltran
RF	Tony Oliva	Roberto Clemente
DH	Jose Canseco	Edgar Martinez
SP	Luis Tiant	Jose Berrios
SP	Camilo Pascual	Javier Vazquez
RP	Livan Hernandez	Javier Lopez

TOP TEN POSITION PLAYERS

	Catchers	1B	2B
1.	Johnny Bench	Lou Gehrig	Jackie Robinson
2.	Yogi Berra	Albert Pujols	Joe Morgan
3.	Roy Campanella	Eddie Murray	Rogers Hornsby
4.	Carlton Fisk	Hank Greenburgh	Rod Carew
5.	Ivan Rodriguez	Stan Musial	Roberto Alomar
6.	Thurman Munson	Jimmy Foxx	Charlie Gehringer
7.	Bill Dickey	Jim Thome	Craig Biggio
8.	Gary Carter	Harmon Killebrew	Ryne Sandburg
9.	Josh Gibson	Willie McCovey	Chuck Knoblauch
10.	Jim Sundberg	Jeff Bagwell	Nellie Fox

	3B	SS	LF
1.	Mike Schmidt	Ozzie Smith	Ted Williams

2.	Brooks Robinson	Phil Rizzuto	Stan Musial
3.	Pete Rose	Pee Wee Reese	Joe Jackson
4.	Ron Santo	Honus Wagner	Barry Bonds
5.	Adrian Beltre	Ernie Banks	Lou Brock
6.	Cal Ripken Jr	Cal Ripken Jr	Willie Stargell
7.	Wade Boggs	Luke Appling	Pete Rose
8.	Pie Traynor	Derek Jeter	Carl Yazstrzemski
9.	Buddy Bell	Bert Campaneris	Rickey Henderson
10.	Graig Nettles	Dave Concepcion	Ralph Kiner

	CF	RF	DH
1.	Ken Griffey	Ichiro	Don Baylor
2.	Willie Mays	Roger Maris	Edgar Martinez
3.	Mickey Mantle	Roberto Clemente	David Ortiz
4.	Tris Speaker	Pete Rose	Harold Baines
5.	Mike Trout	Babe Ruth	Hal McCrae
6.	Kirby Puckett	Tony Gwynn	Paul Molitor
7.	Hack Wison	Joe Jackson	Frank Thomas
8.	Torii Hunter	Frank Robinson	Jim Thome
9.	Duke Snyder	Hank Aaron	Chili Davis
10.	Andre Dawson	Vladimir Guerrero	Mike Sweeney

	RHP	LHP	RELIEVERS
1.	Satchel Paige	Warren Spahn	Trevor Hoffman
2.	Bob Gibson	Sandy Koufax	Rollie Fingers
3.	Nolan Ryan	Steve Carlton	Billy Wagner
4.	Bob Feller	Randy Johnson	Mariano Rivera
5.	Walter Johnson	Tom Glavine	Bruce Sutter
6.	Greg Maddux	Carl Hubbell	Lindy McDaniel

7.	Cy Young	Lefty Grove	Hoyt Wilhelm
8.	Christy Mathewson	Hal Newhouser	Lee Smith
9.	Tom Seaver	Clayton Kershaw	Dennis Eckersley
10.	Roger Clemens	Whitey Ford	Sparky Lyle

PLAYERS WHO DIED DURING THE SEASON

1. Tyler Skaggs, June30, 2019 passed away from unknown causes at this time. I want to dedicate this book to him and all the others that lost their lives as members of the MLB

2. Ray Chapman, August 16, 1920, the only man to die on the field from baseball related injuries. He was beaned (hit in the head) by Carl Mays on the 15th but died the next day

3. Jose Fernandez died in a boating accident on September 25, 2016

4. Nick Adenhart died in a car crash April 9, 2009

5. Josh Hancock also died in a car accident April 29, 2007

6. On October 11, 2006, Cory Lidle died when the airplane he was piloting crashed

7. Darryl Kile died of a heart attack on June 22, 2002

8. Steve Belcher died of a heat stroke in spring training February 17, 2003

9. In another boating accident, March 22, 1993, claimed the life of Steve Olin and mortally injured Tim Crews, who would succumb to his injuries the next day

10. Donnie Moore died of a self-inflicted gunshot wound on July 18, 1989. He had never gotten over the fact that he surrendered a play-off ending homerun the year before

11. Yankee catcher and team captain Thurman Munson died while he was attempting to land an airplane he was piloting on August 2, 1979

12. On August 24, 1979, Lyman Bostock was sitting in his uncle's car when someone in another car pulled a gun and shot him

13. Bob Moose died in a car crash October 9, 1976

14. Walt Bond passed away September 14, 1967 due to leukemia

15. May 13, 1965, Dick Wantz passed away from a brain tumor

16. Tom Gastall drowned on September 20, 1956

17. Tiny Bonham died September 15, 1949 from complications from emergency surgery

18. Willard Hershberger committed suicide on August 3, 1940

19. Len Koenecke was severely injured in a fight on September 15, 1934 (not on the field) and died on the 17th

BASEBALL FIGHTS

It is sad that baseball has some fights/brawls on the field. I believe there should be harsher punishments for those involved, but, hey, that's my opinion.

1.   1911 Ty Cobb went into the stands to get to someone that had been heckling him. The victim had no hands

2.   1923 Babe Ruth punched the umpire in the nose because he disagreed on his balls and strikes, on the first batter. The next pitcher came in, threw out the base runner and continued to throw a perfect game (mentioned earlier)

3.   Juan Marichal and John Roseboro, it involved a bat and Roseboro's head

4.   Pedro Martinez verses Reggie Sanders

5.   Pedro Martinez verses Don Zimmer, Martinez was criticized for this, all he did was push him down, but in a fight you don't walk up to someone and put out your hands as if to grab or hit them. My opinion

6.   Pedro Martinez verses Mike Williams

7.   Pete Rose verses Bud Harrelson

8.   Eric Davis verses Ray Knight

9.   George Brett verses Graig Nettles

10. Thurman Munson verses Carlton Fisk

11. Billy Martin verses Clint Courtney

12. Billy Martin verses Jimmy Piersall

13. Mike Mussina verses Bill Hasselman

14. Bill Dickey verses Carl Reynolds

15. Roger Clemens verses Mike Piazza

16. Bryce Harper verses Hunter Strickland

17. Chan Ho Park verses Tim Belcher

18. A.J. Pierzynski verses Michael Barrett

19. Alex Rodriguez verses Jason Varitek

20. Nolan Ryan verses Robin Ventura, Nolan was nearly twice as old as Ventura, but he showed he had spunk, and Ventura took some lumps

There are tons of fights, one on one and team against team. Totally uncalled for.

I have one question I would like to have someone answer, why does the bullpens all run to the infield fight? I would not do this. (1) Why run all that way just to have to walk back? And (2) Why not just hook it up out there instead of running in and sucker punching someone?

PLAYERS MOST WALKS

A.	Barry Bonds	2,558
B.	Rickey Henderson	2,109
C.	Babe Ruth	2,062
D.	Ted Williams	2,021
E.	Joe Morgan	1,865
F.	Carl Yazstrzemski	1,845
G.	Jim Thome	1,747
H.	Mickey Mantle	1,733
I.	Mel Ott	1,708
J.	Frank Thomas	1,667
K.	Eddie Yost	1,614
L.	Darryl Evans	1,605
M.	Stan Musial	1,599
N.	Pete Rose	1,566
O.	Harmon Killebrew	1,559
P.	Chipper Jones	1,512
Q.	Lou Gehrig	1,508
R.	Mike Schmidt	1,507
S.	Eddie Collins	1,499
T.	Bobby Abreu	1,476

ALL-TIME STRIKEOUT LEADERS

1.	Reggie Jackson	2,597
2.	Jim Thome	2,548
3.	Adam Dunn	2,379
4.	Sammy Sosa	2,306
5.	Alex Rodriguez	2,287
6.	Andres Galarraga	2,003
7.	Jose Canseco	1,942
8.	Willie Stargill	1,936
9.	Mark Reynolds	1,927
10.	Curtis Granderson	1,910
11.	Mike Cameron	1,901
12.	Mike Schmidt	1,883
13.	Fred McGriff	1,882
14.	Tony Perez	1,867
15.	Ryan Howard	1,843
16.	Bobby Abreu	1,840
	Dere Jeter	1,840
17.	Chris Davis	1,819
18.	Dave Kingman	1,816
19.	Manny Ramirez	1,813
20.	Alfonso Soriano	1,803

ALL TIME LEADERS
IN HIT-BY-PITCH

1.	Hughie Jennings	287
2.	Craig Biggio	285
3.	Tommy Tucker	272
4.	Don Baylor	267
5.	Jason Kendall	254
6.	Ron Hunt	243
7.	Dan McGann	230
8.	Chase Utley	204
9.	Frank Robinson	198
10.	Minnie Minoso	192

THINGS I'D CHANGE IF I WERE COMMISSIONER

1. Do away with the DESIGNATED HITTER. Why you ask? (a) it takes away the strategy of the game. Do I let the pitcher stay in or not? (b) it prolongs players careers. That's good? Some players passed the career homer mark and other batting records because they are not good fielders or too slow to be effective and the DH lets them just bat and nothing else

2. Get stricter laws on baseball brawls/fighting. Kids watch these players fighting and think it is the thing to do. It is a DISGRACE to baseball for so much of this. If you want to see people beating on each other go watch boxing, MMA, etc. Keep this unsportsmanlike action of the field.

3. Get rid of INSTANT REPLAY. That is what makes baseball unique. Umpires are people, people make mistakes. People argue "what IF" on lots of calls. I once was calling behind the plate and called a VERY obvious ball a strike. I mean it was obvious, even pre-k kids were telling me it was wrong. I knew it was wrong, BUT, I didn't change my call.

4. Raise the pitching mound back up to where it was before 1968. It was raised to benefit the batter. From the 1880's to

1968 it was the same. Now we can't understand why there is so many home runs, it's the mound. Drop it back down.

5.   Let baseball be what it was in the glory days. I remember even when I was in school, the game was different. If a batter hit a home run, the next batter beware. Or the person that hit the home run.

6.   The brush back pitch should not get the pitcher a warning. As a pitcher, home plate belongs to you, but, as a batter, it belongs to you. Who is backing down? More strategy taken away.

The Baseball Anthology
Editor: Joseph Wallace 1994

The Home Run Encyclopedia
Editors: Bob McConnell and David Wright 1996

Baseball's Hall of Fame: Cooperstown
By: Lowell Reidenbaugh 1983, 1986, 1993

Team By Team Encyclopedia of Major League Baseball
By: Dennis Purdy

Workman Publishing 2006
Big Book of Basball
By: Rob Neyer 2003

Shades of Glory
By: Lawrence D. Hogan

National Geographic
100 Years of the World Series
By: Eric Enders

Sterling Publishing Co., Inc.
The Yogi Book
By: Yogi Berra

Workman Press 1998
Pennant Races: Baseball at it's Best
By: Dave Anderson

Galahad Books 1994
Baseball: An Illustrated History
By: Geoffrey C. Ward and Ken Burns

Alfred A Knopf 1994
The Baseball Book
Editor: Rob Fleder

Sports Illustrated 2011
Baseball Hall-of-Fame
By: Gerald Astor

Prentice Hall Publishing 1984

WIKIPEDIA

GOOGLE

ABREVIATIONS TO ASSIST YOU IN READING THIS BOOK

MLB   =   Major League Baseball

AA   =   American Association

NL   =   National League

AL   =   American League

NNL   =   National Negro League

NFL   =   National Football League

NBA   =   National Basketball League

NCAA   =   National Collegiate Athletic Association

P   =   Pitcher

C   =   Catcher

1B   =   First Base

2B   =   Second Base

3B   =   Third Base

SS   =   Short Stop

LF   =   Left Field

CF   =   Center Field

RF   =   Right Field

SP   =   Starting Pitcher

RP   =   Relief Pitcher

DH   =   Designated Hitter

PH   =   Pinch Hitter

PR	=	Pinch Runner
MGR	=	Manager
GM	=	General Manager
AB	=	At Bat
H	=	Hits
D	=	Double (two bagger)
T	=	Triple (three bagger)
HR	=	Home Run (dinger, long ball, homer, gopher ball, and other nicknames)
GRSL	=	Grand Slam
SB	=	Stolen Base
CS	=	Caught Stealing
Sac	=	Sacrifice Hit
SF	=	Sacrifice Fly
BB	=	Base On Balls (walk, free pass)
IBB	=	Intentional Base On Balls
HBP	=	Hit by Pitch
HB	=	Hit Batter
WP	=	Wild Pitch (error on pitcher)
PB	=	Passed Ball (error on catcher) [the last two the pitcher will blame the catcher or vice versa]
WP	=	Winning Pitcher
LP	=	Losing Pitcher
SV	=	Save
HD	=	Hold
Po	=	Picked Off
DP	=	Double Play
TP	=	Triple Play
AS	=	Assist

Printed in the United States
By Bookmasters